800 DAYS

Gregory Hock

800 DAYS

OVER 300,000 ACCOUNTANTS QUIT
DURING THE PANDEMIC
—HERE'S OUR STORY

To Cheryl,
for your love, support,
and understanding, without which
this book would not have been possible.

CONTENTS

PROLOGUE

As I reflected on the past three years in early 2023, it seemed much had changed. Half of our staff from three years ago were no longer with us. I had not been back to work in the office, or even seen many clients, in three years. It felt dreary.

Many of the changes were a direct result of COVID. Outdoor dining. Fewer employees at most business establishments. Zoom calls.

But changes in the accounting profession had begun years before . . . COVID simply sped it up by dramatically revealing the cracks that were already there. Accountants were clearly not happy with their work.

Long hours and pressure from clients, peers, bosses, and the government. Then even longer hours.

Accounting has always been a pressure-packed profession . . . at least during my forty years. Tax seasons with hundred-hour weeks were not uncommon. There are other professions with hundred-hour weeks, such as investment banking, consulting, and law, but the financial rewards were typically greater in those.

Then there were IPOs. The story goes that during an IPO of a company (one that I later went to work for), three accountants died (or two accountants and an attorney, depending on who was telling the story). One was from a drug overdose, another stroked, and the third jumped off the Golden Gate Bridge.

I could never verify it but have no reason not to believe it. Many in my generation expect to work this hard.

A popular Proverb describes a cup that runneth over. Generally, this is a reference to blessings. Work is a blessing, and accountants have a lot of it. But when we have too much, we cannot keep it in the cup, get it done, or get it done properly and in a timely manner. And when the cup runneth over 365 days a year, it feels like we are drowning.

Back in the '80s, everyone thought we (accountants) would be replaced by computers. In my opinion, computers have had the opposite impact. Without technology, it would be impossible to prepare today's tax returns manually. Technology has set the table for the increasingly complex tax system.

Technology has *increased* the amount of work we have. For example, we see many more computer-generated IRS notices these days than we saw forty years ago—or even fifteen years ago. Unlike larger firms or other professions, many of us with smaller clients don't like to bill for things that are not the fault of our clients. Like an erroneous IRS notice or amending a tax return because a client received a corrected 1099 form. It's more work, but not more money.

One of the biggest impacts on the tax profession and tax seasons happened when somebody decided that the 1099s that brokerage firms file no longer had to be mailed by January 31 each year (like other 1099s). In earlier times, most of our clients had the bulk of their tax information by the first week of February. They came in, and tax season was off and running for ten weeks. Remember that—ten weeks.

The pressure to produce accurate 1099s in less than thirty days (from year-end) proved to be too much. Every year, it seemed, more and more clients began receiving *corrected* 1099s weeks and even months later (after the original was received). If the corrections were big enough, we needed to amend the previously filed returns, often before April 15, to avoid penalties. More work that was not the clients' fault. Inevitably, clients began to wait for their corrected 1099s before scheduling their tax appointment (in March). Finally, somebody said, "Let's get rid of the January 31 deadline and send them out correctly in the first place!"

Since most of our clients have brokerage accounts and get 1099s, our tax season now really begins in mid-March. Tax season (the time to prepare most of the returns or calculate extensions) was now five weeks instead of ten. More work, less time. The result is that tax season with all of the extended returns drags out to mid-October.

Today, younger accountants have a different work-life balance expectation than my generation did. I suppose my parents thought mine was different than theirs as well. The problem is that the accounting profession simply does not meet expectations for the life balance many seek today. And it is getting worse.

Back to the full cup. No single thing made the cup overflow. Not even ten things or a hundred, for that matter. It's been a constant drip, drip, drip. I describe it as death by 1,000 cuts.

As I reflected and went back through my calendar and notes, I realized I did not take a day off for over 800 straight days. I've asked around at conferences and found this was not uncommon.

My objective in writing this book is to help the general public—including our clients and friends—understand what is happening to a wonderful and much-needed profession. COVID was a tough period. My heart goes out to healthcare providers and first responders. I would not want to trade places with any of them. But there were many other COVID casualties as well. By bringing attention to the challenges my profession faced, I hope to encourage change and a revival before the field becomes a casualty. During COVID, 20 percent of all professional accountants left the profession. As I write this, *The Wall Street Journal* published an article titled, "Accountant Shortage Hits Corporations." Many readers may not understand how much of their lives depend on accountants and the work they perform. Without them, how would taxes be calculated and collected? How could the stock markets exist without the tireless work accountants and auditors perform? And so much more.

I hope you and I can be a part of the solution!

I

Ground Zero

CHAPTER 1

NUMBERS DON'T LIE

As of May 2022, there were 5,465 active satellites zipping around the earth in a variety of orbits, the most common being low earth orbit, or LEO.

It's here where the bulk of the surveillance satellites are found—the ones that are constantly taking pictures of every inch of our planet. These satellites, largely unavailable to civilians, discovered some interesting trends starting in August 2019.

Wuhan, the capital of Hubei Province, is known to be the origin of the COVID-19 virus that swept the world. In the later parts of the summer and into the fall that year, long before the virus was even declared to exist, satellites began to notice an increase in traffic to the area hospitals. The parking lots for these Wuhan hospitals were becoming increasingly busier.

Any information that comes in or out of the People's Republic of China is closely monitored and guarded. Accusations of a new pneumonia-style virus were staunchly denied until the virus had been detected far beyond the Chinese borders.

Throughout that fall, information began to leak. Riverboat tours through Wuhan changed routes without explanation. Reports of a novel coronavirus were scarce, and infection rates were greatly underreported.

Amirouche Hammar, a forty-three-year-old resident of Paris, woke up late on December 26, 2019. A headache that developed the evening before intensified overnight and the issues seemed to spread to his lungs. Annoyed that he would come down with a cold over the holidays, he took some painkillers and went to bed early that night.

The next morning, however, his condition worsened. Now with a fever, a dry cough, and shortness of breath, it wasn't a matter of toughing it out any longer. As he displayed classic symptoms of pneumonia, his wife drove him to the emergency room, where he was admitted to the hospital.

At this time, Europe had yet to register official cases of this coronavirus. There was no reason to suspect anything other than a viral infection of the lungs. And it wasn't until a month later, when his fluids were retested, that it was confirmed that Hammar indeed had one of the first European cases of COVID.

By December 31, 2019, suspicions were aroused throughout the world, and Taiwan sent an email to the World Health Organization asking about the patients falling sick in Wuhan. That email, consisting of just four sentences, became a controversial matter. The WHO largely disregarded it. Reports from China denied anything was going on. But people were getting sick, and this disease was spreading far faster than anyone realized.

In late January, an elderly Chinese man from Hong Kong flew to Tokyo after visiting Shenzhen in the Chinese Guangdong Province. Shenzhen, located hundreds of miles south of Wuhan, is a densely packed urban area adjacent to Hong Kong.

From Tokyo, he boarded the Diamond Princess cruise ship out of their Yokohama port on January 17. Two days into the multi-week journey, he developed a cough that gradually worsened.

With his symptoms not diminishing, he ended his cruise early as the ship docked in his home city of Hong Kong just six days after his illness had crept in. Without him aboard, the cruise ship continued its journey throughout the Asian islands and eventually docked in Taiwan on the 31st of that month. It was here that the ship received word from Hong Kong's Department of Health that the elderly man who had disembarked the previous week tested positive for COVID-19. Over the next few days, more and more passengers fell ill until the entire ship was quarantined.

The world, however, still didn't know what was coming.

CHAPTER 2

NEVER HAD A CHANCE

To the outside world, it appears that very little is happening in the tax world during January. Bookkeepers are busy putting together payroll returns, 1099s, and W2s, and closing the books on businesses that shut down the previous year—January is actually incredibly busy for payroll services and bookkeeping. Accountants, tax preparers, and the IRS are all gearing up, getting updates, and implementing last-minute procedural changes.

Accountants make sure their systems and processes are in order. They get things lined up, double-check their software, learn the laws that will change reporting for that tax season, and start sending out letters and emails to clients to remind them that when their paperwork comes in, to get it over to the firm so they can prepare their returns as quickly as possible.

The IRS is working to understand the laws that Congress had changed the previous year, but nothing is final until Congress reconvenes at the end of January. Often, at that time, laws will be passed; many of them are retroactive and will affect the taxes due for the previous year. Once that happens, forms are updated and tax reporting software will ultimately be updated to reflect the changes.

Nothing can really kick into gear, however, until sometime in February.

Firms, like my own, jump into mandatory sixty-plus-hour workweeks as soon as the Super Bowl is over. What none of us knew in early 2020 was that this tax season would be like no other—none of us really had a chance.

CHAPTER 3

ALOHA

Years ago, as my accounting firm was expanding, we purchased several other firms that were closing shop. During those mergers, we acquired a number of new clients. Many of them didn't have another accountant to go to, so they opted to let us manage their accounts going forward. It's pretty standard and happens often as accountants shift, change, retire, or otherwise leave the profession.

Mark and Joanne became my clients that way back in the 1980s.

I wouldn't say that Mark and I were friends, as we didn't get together on the weekends or otherwise spend time outside of a business setting. But we weren't just two acquaintances, either. In the world of accounting, many of us are numbers people, introverted, and logical thinkers. My idea of a good time isn't big crowds and barbeques but rather quiet time with our family. But my clients hold a special place, and I care about them more than just the fact that they keep the business afloat. I have found that most accountants hold a unique bond and sense of responsibility for their clients.

For many people, their accountant is their most trusted advisor. We take this role seriously and maintain a deep sense of protection for them. Regardless of the depth of the relationship, we're in a role where we are responsible for their financial future. That means even if we aren't best friends, we get to know each other fairly well and there's a sense of duty to help them maintain their success.

Over the years as I got to know Mark better, I learned that he and Joanne owned seven different timeshares in Hawaii. As a retired optometrist, Mark and his wife had the resources to enjoy the life they had built. And for them, that was to head across the Pacific and spend multiple weeks every year on the Hawaiian Islands.

Almost as soon as the winter was over, Mark would begin to plan the next trip. Starting in October, they would spend a week at one timeshare, then pack up and head across the island to the next. When that week was up, a small plane would island hop them to the third timeshare until it was time to come home. Back in California, they would stay for a month or two and then head back to Hawaii and do it all again at the remaining four units.

The fall of 2019 was tough . . . Joanne had passed away earlier in June. After battling cancer for many years, she succumbed to the illness. Mark, in her honor, decided that he wouldn't change their plans. He would keep going to the timeshares, keep up the traditions, and honor his wife.

Nobody (outside of the hospitals in Wuhan that were seeing an influx of patients with a strange pneumonia-like virus) had a care in the world about an impending pandemic. Just like the night before Pearl Harbor was attacked, and nobody had a clue that danger was coming, the virus was stealthily making its way out of Asia and into the rest of the world.

CHAPTER 4

WHO'S ON FIRST?

The World Health Organization (WHO) is a specialized international agency put together by the United Nations. Taxpayers from countries around the world contribute over $2 billion annually (the largest chunk of change coming from the USA). The goal of the agency is to be on top of crises that affect public health on a global level. To be able to act quickly, mitigate issues, and help those who are affected by pandemics.

January 2020. Who could not see this coming? Or perhaps I should say, the WHO certainly did not see this coming (or if they did know, they kept it to themselves). Some people did. I did. Numbers don't lie. Every day on the news, the number of people with this mysterious pneumonia increased. As did the number of countries that reported citizens falling ill. The numbers seemed to grow geometrically. But since it started in China, I assumed the numbers were actually much higher, and, in my mind, I suspected they were not growing geometrically but exponentially. It was just a matter of time. It didn't have a name.

Despite evidence that there were people falling ill from months earlier, some from as far back as the summer of 2019, the WHO was relatively silent on the matter. Nobody was raising an alarm; nobody was assessing the risks. Not outwardly, anyway.

President Trump was suspicious that those working at the World Health Organization weren't fully doing their jobs or perhaps they were being influenced by China to keep this thing under wraps. He even went on record in 2020, claiming that a "China-centric" WHO dropped the ball on making sure that everyone was prepared and safe from this deadly, global pandemic. This, after all, is one of the primary purposes of the international agency—they are the organization that is responsible to stop this from happening or to protect us when it does.

It wasn't until the very end of January that the agency finally declared a public health emergency, stating that the outbreak was a "Public Health Emergency of International Concern (PHEIC). Despite the rapidly growing numbers around the world, along with reported cases (and subsequent deaths) increasing exponentially, it would still be another forty-one days before the WHO would call the spade a spade and officially declare COVID-19 to be a global pandemic.

CHAPTER 5

PARTY? WHAT PARTY?

For those who put in the hours to make sure tax preparation is done on time, the days following Tax Day in mid-April are cause for celebration. At my accounting firm, we throw a big party and invite everyone from our multiple office locations to join the festivities and celebrate another successful season.

When January draws to a close, we largely have these events planned, and all that is left to do is book the venue. Normally, Jane, my business partner's wife, will organize these events and run them by the partners to confirm before booking. This is especially true when there are sizable deposits required.

In February, as COVID found its way to the USA and cases were rapidly rising, the hospitality industry noticed that they would quickly be hit hard. Many hotels and event venues put out the notice that if you booked with them, the deposit was nonrefundable. COVID was a hot topic in the news, travel was beginning to be restricted, and a significant number of people were beginning to have concerns about whether this pandemic would have a widespread impact.

"Everything is planned, we're ready to go. We have to put our deposit on the venue as soon as possible so we don't lose the space," Jane said as she gave me the brief on what we should expect for this year's after-tax party.

I looked at her and said, "There won't be a party this year, everything is going to shut down."

Jane looked up from her notebook and raised an eyebrow. "Shut down?" she asked. "Shut down from what?"

Most people weren't following the numbers the way I did; I'm an accountant, after all, and my healthy obsession with numbers allowed me to focus on those trends with keener insight to the pandemic that others didn't have. For over a month, I had been keeping track of cases and where things were heading and could more-or-less see that the USA was the next country in line to get hit hard. I explained, "COVID-19 is already putting a damper on things. Travel is being restricted, the hospitality industry is concerned, and I don't think it's wise to put such a large deposit down for an event space we won't be able to use."

Jane wasn't buying it. This was still a mild concern here in the USA, and just like SARS, the bird flu, the swine flu, and many of these other scares that come around every couple of years, she believed there wasn't really a cause for concern. She did, however, agree to poll the employees (especially those who would be traveling to join us for the after-tax party) to assess their level of concern before pushing the issue any further.

Most of them didn't feel safe in February, and if this thing kept progressing like I knew it would, even if venues were open in April, they *really* wouldn't feel safe at that point.

We didn't book the venue, and there was no after-tax-day party that year.

CHAPTER 6

TRUSTED ADVISOR

Accountants are a unique bunch. Many of us (myself included) are introverts and prefer not to socialize too much. I have a unique relationship with many of my clients in that we are more than just work associates, but we aren't exactly friends. Accountants care deeply about the well-being of our clients—these people put their trust in us, and it's our nature to protect them, but it's not a friendship relationship.

Some accountants who have been in the business for more than a few years prefer not to have our friends as our clients. If you are brand new to the industry, and you need all the clients you can get, you turn to friends and family. Inevitably, however, that leads to taxes and other financial topics coming up when out to dinner or gathering for a meal or drinks. It's just easier to keep business and friends separate to avoid being sucked into "talking shop" whenever you're together.

Because of the necessary trust built into a relationship where an accountant handles your finances, a bond is built, sometimes on little more than just the fact that the accountant handles your finances.

For more than twenty years, I had a client who lived in Washington, DC. We talked a few times over the phone, but we never met in person. I received a call one day from the Alzheimer Unit in a DC hospital, explaining that this client had been admitted to the dementia ward. My reaction was to express my sympathy, but the hospital staff went on to explain that I had been listed as this individual's disability trustee. That trust and bond were so strong that he wanted me to handle his finances when he was no longer able to do so himself.

Mark and I had a similar relationship. Although we lived closer to each other than my DC client, who was literally on the other side of the country from me, we were able to meet for lunch on a handful of occasions, largely building a relationship established through the trust of handling his finances.

In 2005, Mark and Joanne came into my office for an update meeting to make sure their taxes were in order. As we got everything rolling, Mark pulled out a package of folders from his bag.

"Greg," he began, "Joanne and I discussed things, and we know that we aren't in our youth anymore. We don't have children, we don't have any siblings, and our parents are long gone. As our accountant, you know our situation better than anyone else. Would you be the executor of our estate, should anything happen to us?"

He slid the package across the desk to me.

I was caught a little off-guard, but I replied, "Sure, I can handle that for you."

"Thanks so much. Everything you should need as the trustee, or executor, should be in that bundle of paperwork. It includes our will and copies of any other important documents you might need to help wrap things up when the time comes."

We made sure to get power of attorney documents signed, and I slipped the package into my safe deposit box the next time I was at the bank. I thought nothing of it until a decade and a half later.

SUMMARY OF SECTION I

Long before COVID spread throughout the world, it was making its way into the world. Long before most of us even had a clue what was happening, people were getting sick. It seems that many of those in charge tried to keep it under wraps—perhaps they were hoping that it would all just go away before it became a problem.

Later on, while the pandemic was in full tilt, Michael Lewis authored a book called *The Premonition*. This book points out that there were plenty of clues as to what was coming. But censorship and the for-profit healthcare system ensured that the clues were quietly ignored until it was too late.

Many people were actually out-of-sorts because they saw what was coming. There were just not enough of them.

II

Day 1 - Day 39

CHAPTER 7

TOO LATE

February 2020. Looking back on how COVID progressed throughout the world, we see that by February 2020, that snowball was already rolling downhill, gaining size and speed rapidly. There was nothing anyone could do to stop this; all we could have hoped for was to mitigate some of its severe effects. Some speculate that if we had locked down earlier, we could have cut the first wave death toll in half. But that's all speculation, and we can't really know that.

By this point, we saw what was happening around the world. Despite knowing that it was an issue, we didn't even have a way to test for COVID yet; the CDC and FDA were working quickly to approve test kits, but we didn't even have cases in the USA yet. We didn't even have a name for it until February 11, when it was finally announced by the World Health Organization that this disease was now known as the novel coronavirus outbreak: COVID-19.

It wasn't even the end of February when reported cases exploded. Every news outlet was covering the event, we were watching as it came to the USA in droves, and before the end of the month, Italy became a hot spot.

The world watched as Europe turned from historical cities bustling with activity to ghost towns. Nobody was allowed out, and basically the only activity you saw were sanitation crews in hazmat suits spraying disinfectants in public areas.

Death tolls were into the thousands worldwide, the first US death was reported, and countries around the world were reporting their first cases. We were along for the ride now; COVID had gripped the world and would essentially need to run its course—getting much worse before anything could get better.

CHAPTER 8

SIXTY HOURS

In the tax prep world, things don't heat up quickly in February like they used to. It has been like that since the early 2000s when some financial laws were changed.

Previously, 1099 statements, and even some other statements that showed interest or capital gains, were sent right away in January. Clients would receive them and then get a jumpstart on filing their taxes. Then, later, when these companies that issued the 1099s had a chance to look things over, they would send a corrected 1099. These corrected 1099s often would come mid-February or even into March. This meant the client now had to pay to file an amended return.

As clients caught on to this and realized that the 1099 would likely be reissued, they wouldn't even come in until they knew for sure that they had the correct 1099. So they weren't coming in early February anymore; instead, they would wait until March—ultimately compressing the tax season from ten weeks down to four to six weeks.

This confusion led to laws changing, where now the 1099 isn't required to be sent immediately in January. It means that aside from some simple returns, usually those that are just W2s and relatively uncomplicated, the bulk of our tax work gets going after February.

For our accounting firm, the day after the Super Bowl, we move to sixty-hour workweeks. While it is "required" that every tax preparer puts in the hours, it's more of a formality since they would never be able to get through the workload in fewer hours than that.

February of 2020 was starting out to be no different of a year. I was watching the number of COVID cases rise; something was coming down the line, but without any clear instruction from the WHO, the CDC, or even the US government, it was pretty much just life as usual.

My wife and I returned from vacation in January; I got ready for a full cup and started buckling down in February to work long hours for the next two and a half months . . . little did I realize that it would be more like extra-long hours the next two and a half years.

CHAPTER 9

TOO BUSY TO NOTICE

Life is busy. Most of the time, many of us put our heads down, place one foot in front of the other, and just move forward.

Ramping up for the accounting busy season, every tax preparer around the country goes through these same motions. You know it's coming, so you put your head down and push forward. Most years it's busy, it's stressful, and it comes to a close in the middle of April. There's a cumulative sigh of relief, and "Out-of-the-Office" signs are hung as preparers take a much-needed vacation.

This year, I could tell, would be different. While most of the world was too busy to notice what was going on, I was diligently watching the numbers grow. Something big was going to happen; we didn't quite know how it would affect our lives yet.

On February 16, I headed down to Costco. It was a Sunday afternoon, my only day of the week that I could justify taking off. I loaded up my cart with foods and supplies that I never imagined myself purchasing. These were the types of things that you would keep in your garage or basement to be ready in the event of an apocalypse-type tragedy. Foods that would last essentially forever.

While checking out, one of my former employees and her husband were also finishing up their shopping. Their cart looked like a normal Costco run; mine looked like something out of an episode of *Doomsday Preppers*.

"Uh, what's with the stockpiling?" Cassandra asked, nodding toward my cart.

I explained, "COVID's moving fast, and I'm just getting ahead so when the pandemic does hit, I'm not worried."

Cassandra and her husband both raised an inquisitive eyebrow. "The pandemic?" she replied. "I think you're a bit too worried about it. There have hardly even been any cases in the US."

"I think it's coming a lot faster than we think. Either way, I'd rather have these on hand and not need them, than wonder how I'll eat if things do get bad."

I finished checking out and encouraged the couple to take care. I could tell from the looks on their faces that they clearly thought I had lost my mind. To be honest, I hoped I was wrong. If things did get as bad as they looked like they were heading, I might not have stocked up enough.

For the rest of February, life was normal. We kept our heads down, and all twenty-four staff continued to show up and work through the tax preparations as we do every February. One foot in front of the other . . . until we were told we couldn't.

Little did I know that in four weeks, just about everything I had purchased at Costco that day would be wiped from the shelves as millions of people also prepped for the worst.

CHAPTER 10

WHO'S IN CHARGE?

Epidemiologists study diseases. They look at causes, distribution, how the disease spreads, and what can be done to control them. Most people had never even heard of this profession before 2020, and by the middle of February, it was on the tip of everyone's tongues.

News reports talked about the "latest epidemiological reports" and interviewed the top epidemiologists to get a feel for what was actually happening with this novel coronavirus. Too many people, despite being trained professionals and having dedicated their careers to studying diseases, simply did not know.

On February 11 and 12, the WHO organized a Global Research and Innovation Forum. Three hundred of the top experts gathered together, and 150 more joined in via web conference (Zoom was around but still hadn't become a household name by this point). With 450 disease experts brainstorming, they sought answers. What were the gaps? How do we prioritize research?

What measures will we put into place to ensure that knowledge is open to everyone?

These forums, lasting two full days, sought to discover the origins of the virus, how it spreads, how it has been managed in China (remember, it was probably around for six to eight months by this point), how to prevent infection, how can we research a new virus without human testing, and more. One of the most important considerations, less about the virus and more about humans, is how we integrate social sciences into the study. How do we predict what a virus will do, based on what we know about human behavior?

With as many people convening on one topic, it's hard to imagine that nobody had a clue what was going on, where the virus was going, and how to stop it. But as we mentioned before, the WHO has been notoriously slow to respond; this virus was going to devastate the world if they didn't skip the bureaucratic red tape and take action.

It would still be four weeks before the World Health Organization finally announced that it was a global pandemic.

On February 24, the WHO-China Joint Mission on COVID-19 held a press conference to release some of their social findings. What the world already knew was that a deadly virus was spreading rapidly. What we didn't know was how we should respond or how people even would respond.

To sum everything up in just five words: "The world is not ready."

Not ready how, though? No matter what aspect you look at, nobody was ready. Communities were not ready in their mindset on how to deter or eliminate this virus. Economies were not ready with the financial impacts the virus would impose. Hospitals were not ready for the influx of sick and dying people. People were not ready to handle the sudden, and forced, change to how they lived.

In an effort to prepare the world, this press conference stressed the importance of "non-pharmaceutical public health measures." In other words, means of controlling the virus that don't involve vaccines.

This was the first the world had heard about isolation, social distancing, contact tracing, and quarantining. Now the struggle was to garner the attention of seven-plus billion people, get them all on board, and hope that community leaders would take the appropriate measures to keep people safe.

With instructions on how every country should respond, we had a better understanding of what to expect, but we still had no idea when or how bad it would be.

CHAPTER 11

BUREAUCRACY AT ITS BEST

Bureaucracy. Just the word can cause such reactions as groans, eye rolling, and a deep feeling of dread, knowing that when something needs done, you will have to cut through a whole lot of red tape just to get an answer.

By February 2020, the IRS—one of the most heavily bureaucratized organizations in the world—knew full well that COVID-19 was a problem and the impacts were growing in severity every day. Because everything this government organization does is transparent, we can all go back through and look at what they were talking about in the offices. Memos, emails, newsletters, and more all indicate that there were procedures in place for an event like COVID . . . yet when things really started to get bad, it was as though nobody knew what to do.

The Office of Personnel Management (OPM) oversees a large number of government organizations regarding how offices should be run. Think of it like an enormous HR department that isn't just in charge of one company but a bunch of different branches of the government.

On February 7, 2020, long before COVID had truly gained its foothold in the USA, the OPM issued a memorandum that outlined the policies and procedures to follow in case of a serious outbreak like COVID. This policy even identified how to reduce the risk to workers with COVID-19 specifically, or any "other quarantinable communicable diseases." There were guidelines on how telework should be done and how administrative leave or other work-related flexibilities should be handled.

It wasn't even a few weeks later when the IRS admitted that COVID-19 is indeed "a quarantinable communicable disease" and that distancing and quarantining should be done to minimize the risk for the entire organization.

In other words: they knew what was coming down the line, they knew how the IRS workforce should handle the virus when it got bad, and they understood the importance of being able to work from home and minimize contact with those who were infected.

But, as we will see, bureaucracy at its finest means knowing what needs to be done but not being able to implement it without a whole bunch of time and headaches.

CHAPTER 12

HOSPITALIZED

Mark had a handful of friends who would keep tabs on him. For the most part, they helped him navigate these later years in life without his wife.

As a retiree who lived alone, Mark would often be gone for a few days at a time, and nobody would think much of it. He did, after all, love cars and drove off to Nevada on his own recently . . . and then totaled his car and made it back home without anyone knowing that he was even gone.

When a few days had gone by without being heard from, it wasn't unusual. Until a few more days went by, and friends started to get worried.

On March 14, his close friends went to his house to check on him.

"Hey, Mark? Everything okay?" Dave called out as he walked into the house.

There was no answer. Mike followed up, saying, "We haven't seen you for a while, thought we would stop by and visit for a bit."

The two looked at each other worriedly. They set off into the house to see where Mark was, if he was there at all.

Rounding the corner, they were shocked to find him lying on the floor of the living room, bleeding from the head. It didn't look like he had been attacked, but it did seem that he had some sort of episode that caused him to pass out and hit his head on the coffee table on his way down. He was rushed to the hospital; he was breathing, but his vitals were pretty weak.

I didn't find out that he was hospitalized for a few more days.

Recently, I had been watching the news. Parking lots at the local hospitals looked as though they had been revamped into trauma units. Tents were set up to deal with the influx of COV-ID patients—it was almost military-like in appearance. While shutdowns hadn't quite started, it was still difficult to even get in as COVID protocols were in place to ensure everyone's safety.

When I learned of Mark's condition and discovered that being the executor of his estate included acting as his medical power of attorney, I decided to call the hospital for information rather than run the risk of visiting in person.

The thing was, however, that they really weren't even testing for COVID yet. Patients would come in with "flu-like" or "pneumonia-like" symptoms. They would be treated as best they could but often would be discharged, or they would pass away, without officially being coded as having COVID-19.

When I was finally able to talk things over with the doctor, I explained that Mark had been treated recently for symptoms similar to Parkinson's disease. He wasn't officially diagnosed, but there were similar symptoms. This led to an official diagnosis of dysphagia (difficulty swallowing), encephalopathy (a broad term for anything affecting the brain), and respiratory failure.

As he recuperated, Mark developed a rattle in his chest and was diagnosed with pneumonia.

Little did any of us know at the time that he would essentially never get back to life outside the hospital.

SUMMARY OF SECTION II

Before COVID caused massive shutdowns across the country, it was here in the US. It was gaining speed, it was too big to stop, and still, people were living life as usual. The news was all over this thing, and it was called by a handful of names. We heard it called the novel coronavirus, the SARS-CoV-2, and finally COVID-19—later shortened by many to just COVID.

Now that it had a name, everyone was talking about it and how quickly it was spreading through Europe. But few cases were in the US, and it was still a phenomenon that few were treating seriously.

By the end of February, however, the CDC claimed that "disruption to everyday life may be severe."

III

Day 40 – Day 74

CHAPTER 13

BLACK THURSDAY

The stock market has its ups and downs, but when news about a virus with worldwide impact hits, people panic and the market reacts.

Imagine standing on the beach. Everything is bright and sunny, and people are laughing and swimming without a care in the world. There's a light breeze, and you're relaxing with the sun on your face. But you notice offshore that clouds are forming. There's no doubt that a storm is coming, but when is it going to hit? How bad will it be? It appears to be growing quickly . . . will you have enough time to pack up and seek shelter?

It was March 11, 2020, when the WHO finally decided to call a pig a pig and announced that the novel coronavirus (COVID-19) was indeed a global pandemic. Economies around the world shuttered at the news, and the Dow Jones Industrial Average (Dow) showed the fear investors had. On Thursday, March 12, 2020, the Dow dropped by 9.99 percent in a single day—the largest drop since the Black Monday crash back in 1987. Black

Thursday, as it turned out to be, was just the beginning of the tumultuous market season. Just two business days later, Monday, March 16, 2020, saw the Dow dipping by another 12.9 percent.

The biggest difference between the 1987 crash and the one from March 2020 was the recovery. The government acted quickly and pumped a lot of money into the US economy (and a lot of nightmares into the lives of accountants). The market bounced back to pre-pandemic levels in just a couple of months. That bounce back, however, didn't come without a price.

Around the world, nobody really knew what was happening, but if we "follow the money," we can see that uncertainty was everywhere.

Would this new virus be done and over within just a few weeks, like we kept hearing?

If so, why were new travel bans being issued? Why were stay-at-home orders beginning? Why were cruise ships quarantining passengers (for what turned out to be many weeks)?

But even more concerning was the question about whether the market crash was a result of the WHO raising the alarm. Or would the market have crashed regardless of COVID-19 being officially called a pandemic?

The world was in chaos, the stock market was in chaos, and people were scared, uncertain, and worried. And this was just the beginning.

CHAPTER 14

ESSENTIAL WORKERS

Until March 16, official shutdowns had not yet begun. In the week leading up to the 16th, many businesses around the country had the option to keep working in person or to move to a remote working environment.

Our accounting firm has multiple locations. Many years ago, we moved the vast majority of our documents into the cloud. This meant we didn't have to worry about servers, storing documents in person, or having trouble accessing anything from a remote location. It was a fortuitous decision that allowed us to be ahead of the game when remote work became a possibility . . . and eventually a mandate.

Most of the staff in our offices had few barriers to being able to work from home—barring the fact that spouses and kids would be home as well, and we'd yet to see how that would impact lives around the country. The most difficult obstacle to overcome was merely an equipment issue. That was easily solved with a laptop.

The move ended up saving our firm a lot of money. The lease on one of our office buildings was set to renew at the end of 2020. As of late 2019, we had been in negotiations with the building owner, as the rent was going to nearly double upon renewal. When the opportunity to work remotely popped up, our staff jumped on it. With nobody even going into the office, it was an easy decision to simply not renew the lease at the inflated price.

Working remotely, however, did have its drawbacks. We had clients that had been with us for thirty years or more. They were old-school; they didn't have the desire (much less the ability or know-how) to scan all of their tax documents onto the computer and email them to us. They preferred to drop everything off. With an office that was closed, there might have been an accountant there, but the doors were locked and not open to the public.

Accountants being allowed to go into the office was only made feasible by the idea that some workers could be titled "essential workers." They were those who had to keep working in order to keep society (and the economy) functioning. From truck drivers to grocery store workers to healthcare providers, the term "essential" had a wide range of definitions.

So, when an accountant wanted to work from the office rather than from home, or if a client wanted to drop off paperwork in person, they simply said they were essential and were allowed to be out.

Those laws varied from state to state, and even if anyone asked, there was no formal way to determine who truly was "essential."

CHAPTER 15

TOTALED

As I mentioned in Chapter 3, accountants make "friends" with their clients, but it could be considered more of a business friendship. Mostly, it involves catching up during the tax season, having lunch together a few times, or other similar gatherings that are mostly business related.

We're amiable, but it's not like we're inviting each other to our kids' graduation parties.

Mark was one of those clients. I knew his finances and cared about him and his wife, but aside from tax and estate planning matters, I didn't know a lot about him. When I learned that he had been admitted to the hospital for pneumonia-like symptoms, I was concerned and started to pay attention to what was going on in his personal life in case his estate would need to be reconciled soon.

Mark had a lot of close friends who were helping him through this time. During our conversations to figure out what was going on and who would need to handle what, his new-ish Audi was brought up.

"Greg, where is Mark's car?" It was a quick phone call from one of Mark's friends; not that I was being accused of anything but rather it was wondering out loud what had happened to the vehicle. "Mark loved that car. He wouldn't have gotten rid of it . . . but it's not at his house and nobody knows where it ended up."

In essence, we were now all on the hunt for Mark's car. Was it stolen? Parked and forgotten? Did he sell it for some reason or another?

Using my power of attorney as the executor of Mark's estate, I started to dig through insurance records to see if I could find anything about traffic violations, repossessions, or wrecks. Eventually, I discovered what had happened.

Mark was showing some preliminary signs of Parkinson's disease. They weren't severe yet, but he was seeing a doctor at Stanford about them. These symptoms could likely impair driving a bit.

It was the middle of January, and while California and Nevada generally have pleasant weather in the winter, the Sierra Nevada mountain range gets plenty of snow as moisture blows in off the Pacific Ocean. Mark had been taking a little road trip in Nevada; nobody really knows why, perhaps just to get away. During that trip, he lost control of the vehicle and totaled it.

I suspect he was embarrassed, because he never mentioned it to anyone. Somehow, he made his way back to California, and before anything could be reconciled with the vehicle, he fell ill and was admitted to the hospital. We didn't know it at the time, but he wouldn't be going home.

By the time I discovered what happened, the news throughout his friend group regarding the missing vehicle had calmed down.

I decided to let it go; there was no sense in bringing up the fact that his vehicle was totaled. Since Mark decided not to tell anyone about it, I decided not to tell anyone, either.

CHAPTER 16

THE PANDEMIC

When the WHO finally declared the pandemic as a global pandemic, everything started to come down the pipeline. It created this perfect storm where new social initiatives, financial legislation, tax laws, and more all went into effect at more-or-less the same time. Any one of these issues on their own wouldn't have been a big deal; all of them together was like the death by a thousand cuts.

Within a week of declaring the pandemic, the White House declared a national emergency (March 13), then a "no sail" order was issued for cruise ships in US waters (March 14), then shutdowns in some states began the next day (March 15), and then on March 17, not even a week after the announcement of a global pandemic, the White House asked Congress to send direct financial relief to all Americans.

This is really where the book begins. It was the start of a long, convoluted, and agonizing process that most people didn't realize was taking place behind the scenes.

Why? Because a multi-year legislation process was suddenly crammed into just ten days.

On March 27, 2020, President Trump signed the CARES Act, opening up $2.3 trillion to be distributed to US citizens via the first of several stimulus checks ($1,200 per adult and $500 per child), boosting unemployment by $600 per week, waiving early withdrawals from 401(k) plans, and initiating the Paycheck Protection Program (PPP).

Why is this an issue for accountants? To understand what happened, we need to look at how tax laws and acts of Congress like the CARES Act get passed.

Most of the time, laws are passed because some group wants something to be repealed, enacted, changed, or otherwise modified. These people (remember, the US considers corporations to be people) pay the lobbyists, the lobbyists call their favorite senators and members of Congress, and then slowly things start to take form.

Finally, someone will draft the legislation, but often it won't go through on its own, so they have to piggyback off another bill that looks good or is more likely to pass. This can take a considerable amount of time.

When the bill does get passed, it includes an effective date, one that few people ever agree on, so they have back-and-forth on when this new bill will be passed into law. Usually, they try to make it reasonable, like January 1, but often they have arbitrary dates to allow certain situations to be grandfathered in.

With tax laws that are changing, industry groups and the IRS start to study it. They have to read drafts and try to figure out the intent behind the new law. Since they're almost never cut-and-dry, the IRS goes through months of public hearings to figure out just how the law will impact every known situation.

In a good year, that can take six months; in a bad year, that's an eighteen-month process.

Finally, the IRS has regulations on how the law is to be interpreted. These regulations aren't law yet, but most of the time, you can rely on them when filing taxes. Congress sometimes has to clarify them and say, "Yes, that was the intent" or "No, you're missing the point." If you filed based on these regulations, and then they "missed the point," audits can come down the line several years later.

Realistically, if the tax law is making a major change and will affect a lot of people in many different financial situations, the entire process can take several years to get all the kinks worked out after tax court cases involving new laws start to be resolved to give guidance on specific issues.

We didn't have that kind of time at the beginning of what turned out to be a very long pandemic period. So, a lot of people worked around the clock to condense the first part of the process—one that takes eighteen months—down to just ten days.

Think of it like you were building a car. Normally, it would take a week to get it done—but in this situation, you've gone start to finish in one afternoon.

On the surface, it sounds simple enough: $1,200 stimulus per person, $600 in bonus unemployment, and a handful of other things to ensure Americans aren't left financially destitute during a time of uncertainty. While that might sound clear, there's a whole lot more to it when you get into the actual accounting side of it.

CHAPTER 17

DO WHAT?!

The IRS is an enormous governmental bureaucracy made up of federal employees. Before COVID hit, this organization was woefully understaffed. But now consider this.

On March 9, the IRS limited all nonessential city-to-city travel for thirty days (remember, we all thought this disease was going to pass much, much faster than it actually did).

On March 16, the IRS started closing facilities as nationwide shelter-in-place orders started to take effect.

On March 21, the IRS extended the tax filing deadline from April 15 to July 15.

On March 26, the IRS closed two of its major processing centers, with the third to close a week and a half later on April 6.

On March 30, the IRS directed all employees to evacuate IRS facilities and work from home (something nearly none of them were even set up to do).

On March 30, the IRS and the Treasury Department announced that distributions of the economic stimulus payments would begin in three weeks. If you had already filed 2019 returns, that information would be used to determine eligibility; if not, then 2018 information would be used.

Here's where the "fun" starts. This organization, understaffed, trying to work from home, in the middle of tax season, was now attempting to figure out how to distribute over one hundred million stimulus checks. This is unprecedented in size and speed for them, but it also set up accountants for an influx of calls from their clients . . . while still trying to work from home and prepare taxes. This doesn't even account for the fact that for the next three months, tax payments would be mailed in (with checks paying taxes owed) to a facility that was unstaffed—literally millions of pieces of mail were piling up and up.

The problems, it turns out, went much deeper than just "use information from the last time you filed taxes." My phone would not stop ringing, and I had no way of calling the IRS (not that anyone would answer and respond to calls anyway) to track down these answers.

"Greg! You need to hurry and get my 2019 return done ASAP! My income is lower this year, and if the IRS uses 2018 information, we don't qualify for a stimulus check . . . oh, and we don't have all the information for our 2019 taxes yet."

"Greg! I've been thinking, we have been claiming my adult son for a few years now. He actually moved out three years ago, but we wanted to keep the tax breaks going. Can we amend our 2018 return and take him off our taxes so he gets the full $1,200 instead of the $500 on ours?"

"Greg! We already filed our 2019 return, and we don't qualify for a stimulus. But we do qualify if we use the 2018 returns. Can we 'un-file' our taxes so we get the stimulus?"

"Greg! We sold our house last year and showed huge capital gains. Normally we would qualify for this stimulus, but that one-time gain throws it off. What are our options?"

"Greg! We got divorced last year. Who is getting the $500 for our kids?"

"Greg! We moved and haven't updated our address with the IRS. How do they know where to send the check?"

"Greg! We closed the bank account connected with our tax returns. How will the IRS direct deposit our stimulus?"

The calls went on and on. With hundreds of clients around the country, there was seemingly no end to these questions. The client couldn't call the IRS (nobody was there to answer), accountants were working from home (which wasn't a big deal if it was just you, but spouses and kids were home as well—how much work was getting done?), and we still needed to prepare hundreds of tax returns before the new date of July 15.

But that raised even more questions.

What about the small business owner that pays quarterly estimates? Are all those estimates delayed until the middle of July as well? How do we even compute quarterly estimates for the first two quarters of the year when we haven't even completed taxes for the previous year?

Are state taxes delayed as well? At this point, the IRS said federal returns weren't due until July 15, but every state makes their own laws regarding state taxes.

Now they throw into the mix more than just the stimulus. And we had to field calls about the 401(k) distributions. Calls like:

"Greg! I heard I can take $100,000 from my 401(k) and not pay taxes. Is that true?" This, by the way, was not true. Penalties were waived, but you still had to pay income tax. This was almost always followed with, "Greg! Does the new waiver-of-penalty rule apply to my state?" Again, we didn't know; nobody had told us how this worked on a state level.

Then came the PPP loans. This was a lifesaver for many clients—in our case, our influx of cash from preparing returns suddenly disappeared in March and April; we needed those loans to keep all our employees. A later chapter will get into the pitfalls associated with these loans.

Finally, what about the accountants who had planned vacations for after tax season? Should they cancel their vacations and try to get refunds? "But I want to go!" If I need to reschedule . . . for what month? These didn't really come to fruition anyway, since the two weeks to a month touted as the timeline before COVID was over ended up being more like two years. But the staff did not know this yet.

The bottom line is that all these new IRS rules extended the worst tax season of our lives for three more months. So long, sixty-hour workweek; hello, eighty-hour workweek. My cup was already full; now it was starting to overflow.

CHAPTER 18

UNEXPECTED CALL

Tax preparers around the country were busy with preparing tax returns on Saturday, March 14. It was the last weekend before corporate and partnership taxes were due on Monday. We had already ramped up to sixty-hour workweeks in my office, and my week looked more like an eighty-hour workweek. Late afternoon, my phone rang.

"Hey Greg? My name is Tim. I'm Joanne's cousin." The caller introduced himself as Mark's wife's cousin. "Mark is in the hospital. His friends found him unconscious on his living room floor. So far, they don't know what's going on."

Neck-deep in tax returns, I didn't want to dismiss him immediately. "Oh no, that's not good. Thanks for letting me know, Tim. I appreciate the call. As you know, I'm the executor and successor trustee, so keep me informed if Mark gets better or he takes a turn for the worse."

"I certainly will. But, Greg, I was going through estate documents, and you're not just the executor and successor trustee.

Mark has you listed as power of attorney for healthcare, and general power of attorney."

I sat in stunned silence for a minute. Mark had me in charge of . . . everything? Finances I can figure out, but healthcare is a topic I'm terribly unfamiliar with.

"You're probably as shocked as the rest of us," Tim went on. "We should probably change the locks on Mark's door to keep things secure. When I was over there, his safe was open; I don't think anything was stolen, but I shut it just in case."

My focus diverted from taxes for a moment, and I informed him, "Certainly, Tim, I'll look into getting locks changed this weekend, and we'll figure out what we need to do. In the meantime, can you pay any outstanding bills? Just keep track of the expenses, and I'll reimburse you from the estate when I'm able."

We made plans to get started with the process, and I mentally prepared myself for my new roles that would essentially become another full-time job. I went back to working on taxes for the rest of Saturday.

Sunday morning came around, and I was on the phone. I placed calls to the hospital to find out details on what happened (nobody knew), and then I started calling locksmiths that could change the locks on Mark's home.

I live about fifty minutes south of Mark. Checking on his estate wasn't as easy as popping in for a few minutes in the afternoon; it was almost a half-day process to get anything done. As I tracked down locksmiths, I quickly discovered that COVID, despite being a day away from official shutdowns, was already shutting things down. Call after call came back with the same response: "Sorry, we're not doing house calls until further notice."

Frustrated, I finally turned to my own connections. A locksmith had done some work on our house and at our office. With that established relationship, I was able to appeal to him about working on Mark's house despite the uncertainties. Of course, it meant paying for nearly two hours of travel to do a simple lock-change job.

By Sunday evening, I had already spent over seven hours dealing with "things" that popped up. With Mark in the hospital and unresponsive, a lot of it was taking our best guesses as to what needed done and where information was to be found.

One of Mark's four closest friends was Pat, a retired nurse. She agreed to be listed as power of attorney for healthcare to help alleviate that part of the burden. Together, the five of us split the duties to clean up Mark's house and find out where his assets were (we were able to locate all of them aside from the Audi he wrecked without telling anyone). We met the neighbors, arranged for mail pickup, and started tracking down service providers like the gardener, house cleaning staff, and anyone else.

In the hospital, Mark was doing "okay" but didn't have a prognosis yet.

For me, it was back to tax work.

CHAPTER 19

BEHIND THE SCENES

By the time March was halfway over, the world was in crisis. Stay-at-home and shelter-in-place orders were issued, the financial markets were in shambles, and nobody had a clue what was going on—or how long this thing would even last.

The government, however, was working around the clock to bring some sort of order to the world and figure out how to stave off a complete economic collapse. Most of the time, bureaucracy only makes things more convoluted and confusing, but I have to hand it to the US government for hitching up their pants and making things happen.

By March 21, the IRS had extended tax deadlines to the middle of July. Not even a week later, the CARES Act was passed. It wasn't something that could be done on a whim; it wasn't something you could crank out by running ChatGPT overnight. This took some dedicated time and effort.

The entire bill is 335 pages long. That's much shorter than most acts or bills, but it still would have required thousands of human-hours to put together. We don't know who all was working on it, where they got the ideas from, or what those sessions looked like, but we can speculate that a huge team was working twenty-four hours a day figuring out all the possible scenarios to push a $2 trillion legislation through.

It propped up the economy, for sure, but it also piled on the work to tax professionals around the country.

Take, for instance, the increase in unemployment benefits. Millions of people were laid off, temporarily or permanently, due to the pandemic. The CARES Act increased their unemployment benefits by $600 per week. Great news if you're unemployed and unsure of when you're going to get back to work.

In any normal situation, that is, outside of the pandemic, sole proprietors and partners in partnerships can't claim unemployment benefits. Unemployment is an insurance with premiums paid through payroll taxes. Sole proprietors and partners aren't employees and thus haven't paid into the insurance pool.

The CARES Act allowed these unqualified individuals the ability to claim unemployment benefits.

The result of this increased unemployment benefit was that the California Employment Development Department (EDD), responsible for overseeing and managing unemployment insurance and benefits, was completely swamped (I work in California, so this is the department we work with most often). In March alone, they had over one million people applying for unemployment, with more to come in the following months.

If that wasn't bad enough, the CARES Act was a federally mandated piece of legislation. It allowed for an increase in unemployment benefits—a state-run program. Essentially, what they were saying was, "Go ahead and increase the benefits, pay out of pocket, keep some good records, and we (the US government) will reimburse you later." If that doesn't sound like a recipe for disaster, just wait for the rest of the fallout.

Of course, now we had unemployed people who technically didn't qualify for unemployment but who were receiving benefits.

Who?

What about those who had a job lined up but didn't start the new job because everything was put on hold?

They didn't qualify for benefits from their old job because they didn't work there anymore. They didn't qualify for benefits from their new job because they hadn't started yet. They did qualify, under this legislation, for benefits . . . but who ultimately paid for that?

And guess who got to field all the questions that arose with anything that had to do with financial matters?

Yep, the accountants who were already just barely keeping their heads above water.

CHAPTER 20

HEAD 'EM OUT

On Sunday, March 15, New York announced they would shut down public schools. 1.1 million students were suddenly forced to learn from home. School districts around the country would follow suit within the next couple of days.

By the end of the next day, the counties where I live and work issued mandatory shutdowns and called for stay-at-home orders . . . orders that were largely unenforced, but most businesses at least temporarily diminished their hours and certainly limited access.

Largely unenforced, however, doesn't mean completely unenforced. One of my clients owns and operates a restaurant. During this time, they met up with a friend to ensure nothing was left out that would spoil—lights were off, doors were locked, just two people in the building. They were issued a citation from the police.

Concerts around the country were canceled.

Church services were closed.

Groups could consist of no more than fifty people—most states would soon lower this to twenty, and then ten.

Masks were encouraged, and it was recommended that we stay at least six feet apart to minimize contact.

With businesses shut down, work-from-home orders were ramping up.

But we were still told that this wouldn't be a long-lasting pandemic. We were encouraged to stay home and give it "two weeks to flatten the curve." Most people believed that within three weeks or a month, all would be back to normal, and many simply looked at this as a forced two-week vacation.

Accountants, however, were not able to do that. We were a month out from the tax deadline (April 15 was still the deadline at this point), and all this did was force tax preparers to work from home, where it was likely much less efficient. For those who didn't have children, it wasn't as big of a deal—merely overcome the inconvenience of not having the convenience of being in an office space. For those tax preparers who did have children, though, they're trying to get work done, manage children, coordinate Zoom calls with teachers, and deal with the added stress and aggravation of working in a chaotic environment.

There would never be a good time for a global pandemic to shut down the country, but for everything to hit a month before the tax deadline, during the busiest time of most accountants' lives, it turned into the perfect storm of inconveniences for tax professionals.

Little did I know at the time, but this was the first week of the most chaotic year of my entire life.

CHAPTER 21

FINAL MEETING

My primary office is about an hour and a half from my house. When I left for work on that Monday (March 16, 2020), it was like any other day going into the office. Obviously, the news was riddled with reports of the coronavirus, new cases, and related events happening around the world.

I turned on the radio to listen to the latest as I drove.

". . . following a 14 percent increase in positive COVID-19 cases in California, Governor Newsom has ordered all residents to shelter-in-place. This order goes into effect at midnight and will last until April 7. You are not confined to your homes; however, you are asked to stay inside unless absolutely necessary . . ."

I can't say that I was shocked, but I was a bit shocked. These stay-at-home orders were in place around the world, but this is America, the Land of the Free. I pondered the information as I finished my drive to the office.

I only had one tax meeting with clients that day (remember—people were just beginning to receive their broker 1099s). The couple came in, and we got down to business despite the pressing unknowns regarding the shutdown. While I didn't realize it at the time, this ended up being my final in-person tax meeting for that year. Going forward, everything would be done on the phone or on a Zoom call.

Until this point, nothing had really changed in my tax world. We were still preparing 2019 tax returns, we were anxiously awaiting the end of the pandemic by the middle of April, and as soon as Tax Day came and went, we expected that life would be back to normal. We were treating April 15 as our "deadline" to get returns completed.

It would be just five more days until laws started changing and we would be hit with a barrage of changes and questions that nobody knew the answers to . . . and there would be nowhere to turn to get the right answers.

But for now, we had plenty of questions. What was going on with this pandemic? What made this worse than other outbreaks like swine flu, bird flu, SARS, and more? Why is it spreading so fast, and what's going to happen?

Furthermore, in-person life was shutting down. Who are "essential workers"? The news was talking about how only essential workers could be out and about; accountants are considered essential workers. But now what happens if you aren't essential and you're out of the house?

We had no parties going on, no church meetings, no concerts, no gatherings at all. But for work, just about everyone could make the claim that they're essential.

Besides that, is there a punishment if you're out and about but you're not performing duties of your essential job? Places like China had severe penalties—punishments for breaking the quarantine rules could land a person in prison for several years.

Without firm answers, we all seemed to enter into a haze, a fog. One where we had to keep trudging forward without knowing what was coming next.

On the way home, I figured I would stop at the grocery store to grab a few things to at least get us through the next couple of weeks. I had already picked up emergency food, in case the situation got really bad. But we needed bread, meat, and a few other everyday staples.

When I walked into the store, most of the shelves were bare. It was almost like the place had been looted, except instead of people running out with armloads of goods, they were lined up, waiting to check out; those lines stretched all the way to the back of the store.

I didn't get any groceries that day. Not that they would have been in stock if I had wanted to wait in those lines.

CHAPTER 22

THE GOLDEN STATE

California is home to one-eighth of the US population. With such a large percent of the population, it's imperative that people are taken care of when a global pandemic is bearing down on us. It was declared that January 25 was Day One for the pandemic coming to the Golden State, and Santa Clara County declared a local health emergency by February 3—more than a month before the WHO finally declared a worldwide pandemic . . . perhaps the WHO should open a recruiting office in Santa Clara County?

By the time March rolled around, most of the country was still operating as usual. Nobody seemed to be concerned except for a few groups that were working hard to ensure public safety. Just as the federal government was putting in long hours so they could, in a matter of days, push through legislation that usually takes years, the California government was working overtime to mitigate the impact of the virus.

By March 4, the governor had declared the virus to be an emergency, setting in motion a series of events that would come one after another in such rapid succession that it was hard to wrap our heads around the changes. This also opened up coronavirus testing to everyone, as insurers were not able to charge for the tests.

A couple days later, Stanford University transitioned all their classes online; the next day, California reported that there were officially one hundred confirmed cases in the state.

When the report dropped that a hundred cases had been confirmed, San Francisco banned large group gatherings. A few days later, Disneyland shuttered their gates. Senior homes closed their doors to visitors by the middle of the month, and on March 16, the Bay Area Counties declared everyone was to shelter-in-place.

Restaurants moved to take-out only—a pivot that was the only saving grace for thousands of small businesses that otherwise would have gone under.

Legislation opened up an emergency $1.1 billion for COVID support, and by the 20th of March, the National Guard had been deployed to help distribute emergency food to those who were otherwise compromised or unable to procure their own.

By the 21st, the state had surpassed 1,200 confirmed cases; twelve times as many as just a couple of weeks prior. This number would increase another six-fold by the end of the month as the disease spread much faster than anyone had imagined. The influx of patients meant that the state had to lease two empty buildings and convert them to hospitals to deal with those suffering.

Banks delayed foreclosures due to non-payment; the DMVs closed, and by the end of the month, over one million unemployment claims were filed.

On March 31, as the month drew to a close, the State Superintendent of Public Instruction told school officials that the schools would be closed for the remainder of the school year.

These issues changed California from normal operations to a complete shutdown in about four weeks.

And most of the population was still under the impression that it would just be a few weeks to "flatten the curve and return to normal."

CHAPTER 23

MISSION CRITICAL

People panicked as businesses shuttered their doors. It wasn't a panic that resulted in riots and widespread looting but one that resulted in confusion, fear, and an overall stalling. Things just stopped, without anyone knowing when they might pick back up again.

For the IRS, it was no different. This enormous government entity closed up shop, saying they would get back at it "when it was safe." Because at the beginning of March, the COVID-19 response plan went into effect and was designed to limit the disruption of services to taxpayers and stakeholders.

It forced the organization to make significant changes to just about every aspect of its operations, right in the middle of tax filing season. They were now making crucial decisions on which facilities would stay open, how many people would remain working, who would work from home, and what operations would be given priority.

With six weeks until Tax Day (which we later learned would be pushed out three more months, causing even more issues), these changes created a huge burden for local accountants.

As all submission processing centers were closed, the organization stopped taking paper tax returns. Now, millions of people around the US didn't know where to send their returns. Who did they call?

Their accountant.

The IRS shut down all of their toll-free taxpayer assistance lines. If a citizen had a question about their taxes, even calling the IRS was no longer an option; so, who did they turn to?

Their accountant.

Because incoming mail wasn't being processed, those who submitted electronic returns but owed money could write a check and send it to the IRS. But that envelope ended up sitting in a warehouse with literally millions more pieces of mail, not to be opened for many more months. The client would receive a deficiency notice saying they hadn't paid their taxes. Now they are wondering if they need to re-file, send a different check, try to pay electronically, or something else. And you know who they called.

Their accountant.

Over the course of a couple months, the IRS would accumulate over sixteen million paper tax returns that needed to be processed. But, at the same time, they had slashed the number of full-time employees. Their overall workforce (in the office) dropped from eighty-one thousand to just three thousand . . . and soon that would drop even more to a mere one thousand employees spending a full week at an IRS facility.

That doesn't mean others weren't "working." It means that the rest of the employees were attempting to work from home.

Remember, there's mass confusion around the country as to what's happening. Every state is responding differently. People are working from home, and their kids and spouses are home as well. Take an IRS employee who isn't set up with a home office, get them to homeschool their kids while they work from home, and then take away all resources, and it's no wonder that mayhem in the tax world would be the result.

That mayhem had to go somewhere. It overflowed into the next most logical place: the accountants' offices.

Now, as the IRS wasn't available, tax preparers and accountants were inundated with phone calls from their clients. Every client had a different question about how this would affect their individual situation. And every client needed an answer . . . but many of the questions didn't have answers.

At this point, my office was already working sixty-hour weeks, I was putting in around eighty hours per week, and I had Mark's estate to deal with, which added another twenty-plus hours—leading to a total of more than one hundred hours of work per week. Now, every client was calling and asking questions; they were calling so fast that I couldn't even hang up the phone before it would ring again. My cup runneth over.

CHAPTER 24

HOME ALONE

Around the country, two hundred million people are suddenly forced to work from home. At first, it wasn't a big deal. It was thought that in two weeks, activities and institutions would start to open back up and we would return to school, work, and life as usual. By the end of March, as the situation continued to get worse, the idea of going back to life as usual looked more and more like a pipe dream than a reality.

For many of us, that two weeks stretched out into nearly two years.

Imagine, if you will, how a typical day went for many of those newly remote workers. Or, perhaps, you lived it and you don't have to use your imagination—instead you can recollect and be quite thankful that we aren't trying to live like that anymore.

Schools were shut down. Teachers, who had no training to deliver remote learning, were forced to teach via Zoom. Children, who had minimal attention spans even when in person, were forced to try to learn via Zoom. In California, schools were closed for the remainder of the 2019–2020 school year, and throughout the entire 2020–2021 year as well. Nearly a year and a half of having kids trying to learn from home.

When life didn't open back up as fast as some thought, the idea that this was an extended "snow day" diminished, and our everyday lives didn't get easier. Instead, they got harder and harder.

Putting in a full eight-plus-hour day of work can be done from home. But parents also have to manage children who are trying to do school from home. When they are done with their schoolwork, it's not as easy as just kids being kids. They had no friends to play with, and most youngsters needed to get their energy out. Video games, Netflix, and other electronic forms of entertainment could only occupy them for so long.

Now, working from home meant eight-plus hours dedicated to the job, and it also meant eight-plus hours dedicated to homeschooling and managing children. Furthermore, it meant dedicating at least a few hours to managing a chaotic household. That left very little time for anyone who wanted to relax, get a good night's rest, or even find a few minutes of solace for themselves.

Consider the fact that many professionals, like accountants, were trying to put in over twelve-hour workdays (on top of the fact that day-to-day tasks were taking three times as long), and something had to give . . . usually it was a good night's rest.

For many people, it would be a dream to be home alone working. For most people, however, there was no "alone" aspect to working from home—their dream was more of a nightmare.

CHAPTER 25

PUBLIC HEARINGS? WEBINARS? CPE?

COVID managed to shut down the world at precisely the most inopportune time—as far as the tax world goes, anyway. There's never a good time to completely stalemate everything, but a month before Tax Day was terrible for us. If we could have just scheduled the pandemic for late October, November would have been a busy month, but it would have made life a little bit easier for accountants and tax preparers.

We talked about how busy everyone was, trying to work from home, manage a household, homeschool kids, and maintain their sanity. But let's dip a bit more into how insane it was if you worked as a tax preparer.

Normally, we see laws change every single year. Many of them apply to taxes; many do not. When a new tax law comes down the line, it's talked about for months and months. There are webinars, public hearings, and seemingly endless opportunities for professionals to learn what's going on and how the new law will apply to just about every scenario possible. Then, even if an accountant managed to skip all that public discourse, they had mandatory continuing professional education (CPE) classes to keep their license—these classes provide the opportunity to learn the new laws.

None of that was available during COVID; the laws changed so quickly that there simply wasn't time.

When the federal government extended the tax filing deadline to July 15, they moved the deadline to pay any taxes owed to that date as well. For many people, this was a welcome relief. With three extra months to get their taxes done, it meant a little longer to figure things out.

For those of us preparing the taxes, however, it caused headaches that would not go away in those three months. The yearly filing date was extended, but what about F-Bars (foreign taxes)? What about quarterly tax estimates that are normally due in June? Will those be extended as well? All these questions resulted in more phone calls, continuing to fill the already overflowing cup.

There was, however, an even bigger question. Federal tax deadlines were extended; were state tax deadlines extended as well? Every state sets their own rules and regulations, and there was no time to get on the phone and call the tax departments for all fifty entities to find out. Even if you did call the tax office for each state, many of them didn't know if they would be extending their own deadlines—if they were even there to answer the phones!

These sudden changes led to the increasing nightmare. When the laws were changed, nobody anticipated all the questions. Normally, that wouldn't be such a bad thing, but this was far from a normal year.

Accountants and other tax professionals were already working extended hours leading up to (the original) Tax Day. Suddenly, there was an announcement about deadline changes, and our phones were ringing off the hook (they already were, but now they were ringing twice as much . . . if that is possible).

Clients were calling to ask how the new regulations would affect their tax situation. Sometimes when the client asked the question, it was the first time we had even heard of the new law; let alone have time to figure out what it even meant or how it would apply to their particular situation.

They all needed answers to questions that had no answers. So, they would eventually ask, "Well, what would you do in this situation?" We could only give our professional opinion and hope for the best. After a half hour on the phone, we hung up, only to have the phone ring immediately with the next client calling in—we could have spent every workday fielding calls.

Of course, there were still tax returns to file, COVID issues to deal with, a company to manage, work-from-home employees who needed equipment, and everything else life-related that had to get done.

If you think an eighty-hour workweek is bad, try one-hundred-plus hours.

CHAPTER 26

TON OF BRICKS

Our profession was just hit with a ton of bricks.

Imagine if you were tasked with drinking 365 gallons of water. If you could spread that out over the course of an entire year, it wouldn't be so bad . . . you would probably actually be healthier for it. Now imagine all that water coming at you at once. Not only are you overwhelmed, but you're also probably knocked down with little hope of getting back up.

Legislation was coming out of DC like a firehose.

For every new piece of legislation enacted that impacted taxes, there were hours of work to go along with them. We had to learn what the law did, how it worked, how it would impact clients, and which clients it would impact. Then, when the clients learned of the new laws, they would call in, wondering what they were supposed to do, and they'd set up Zoom meetings to plan out the next course of action.

Spread out over the course of a month, a new law added up to (maybe) twenty-five extra hours of work.

Within a few days, new laws that affected taxes, tax filing, and more were flung at us: over a hundred new laws that all needed answers immediately.

Naturally, with millions of people laid off, the California unemployment offices were inundated—overrun. The modest staff who were able to stay on were scrambling to make heads or tails of what to do. When a client couldn't get through to them, the client called the next person on the list: their accountant. The accountant, after all, is good with numbers and knows their finances, so they certainly seemed like the right person to answer these questions, right?

No, most accountants aren't familiar with how to file unemployment claims; that's not our job. It's a money issue, but that's about as far as these similarities get.

And now we were receiving calls and emails from not just our clients but their friends and family. A client has a friend who usually files their own taxes. They can't call the IRS because those help lines had been shut down. So the friend, being the good friend they are, said, "I'll just call my accountant and find out for you."

Or perhaps it was a client with grown children who use a different accountant. That adult son or daughter couldn't get through to their accountant, so the parent called us.

Everyone had questions. They turned to the only people they knew who should have the answers. All the while, the IRS was extending the deadline to give three extra months to ensure everything got handled. Remember, at this time, most people still believed that this would all be done and over within a matter of weeks. Although many were starting to get skeptical when the case numbers and deaths just kept climbing.

In the accounting world, your big break comes after April 15. You work hard for a couple of months and then you take a well-deserved, and badly needed, vacation. Those vacations almost always came at the end of April and early in May.

But now that tax season wouldn't end until July 15, what do you do with that vacation that had been planned for months? Employees were stressed that they would miss their vacation, they wondered if their employer would let them take the time off, and shoot, they even wondered if the pandemic would even let them go. If their flight was canceled and the hotel was shut down, would they get a refund on their travel?

All these personal questions were pressing and taking up a big portion of their brain power—at the expense of productivity.

At this time, the financial world ws panicking. Hotel stocks were plummeting, some losing over 50 percent; cruise ship stocks were faring even worse, some of those lost over 80 percent of their value within weeks.

But there was so much more to come.

CHAPTER 27

STANDBY

Mark desperately wanted to go home from the hospital. I can't blame him; living in the hospital is hardly living at all. His fall, combined with the "pneumonia" in his chest (that was possibly COVID, just undiagnosed because it was untested for) and his overall declining health, meant that he wasn't healing as quickly as he had hoped.

Eventually, however, he pleaded hard enough and was able to be discharged from the hospital. Since he couldn't live without medical care, his discharge process created a lot of extra work and zapped already-strained medical resources.

Even though it was technically still "early" in the pandemic, hospitals were being overrun. Many of the local hospitals were setting up tents as temporary morgues to handle the influx of patients who succumbed to this virus. Every bed was spoken for, and temporary beds were necessary so nobody would be turned away.

Meanwhile, I was making calls to find an at-home healthcare company that would be willing to be on standby. According to the hospital discharge, Mark was stable enough to go home (with twenty-four-hour care).

As you can imagine, healthcare workers were strapped. Anyone who could work was already working, and to pull them away from the hospitals and patient care where they were desperately needed would be a tough bargain.

After countless hours on the phone, negotiations, and practically downright begging, the bed and the care company were lined up. But I still needed to find an ambulance that would take time out of their busy schedule to transport Mark home.

That meant even more phone calls during the busy tax season.

We eventually had it all set up. The bed was in place at Mark's house, the care company would be there to meet him when he arrived via ambulance, and a plan was in place to provide care around the clock. With how much his condition had worsened over the past few months, we were hoping for the best, but nobody really had high hopes that this would work out as well as Mark hoped it would.

Upon arrival, Mark was confused. He didn't understand what had happened. He couldn't figure out why the locks were changed on his home. He asked about his wallet and his Audi (you know, the one he wrecked somewhere in Nevada and didn't tell anyone about). His confusion turned to frustration; his frustration turned to anger. He wasn't combative with his caregivers, but he certainly wasn't amiable to them either.

Mark wasn't even home for six hours when he was in an ambulance, heading back to the hospital.

He wouldn't return home.

HYDRO WHAT WITH CHLORINE?

It was late March and the world was scrambling to figure out how to slow the disease. Still, the best that anyone could come up with was to stay home. Don't be around other people, and the virus won't have a chance to spread. There certainly had to be a better way, right?

You may recall that initially, masks were discouraged. At the time, a whole lot of misinformation was going around regarding masks; some of it spread by prominent political figures. In truth, the discouragement to wear masks came at a time when there was a heavy mask shortage—every last one was necessary in the hospitals where people were being actively treated for COVID.

When it became apparent that individuals could be carrying the virus but not showing signs and symptoms, masking became a necessary precaution to dampen the spread of the virus.

Then there were other rumors about a "new" drug that was being used and shown to minimize the COVID symptoms. Hydroxychloroquine sulfate was suddenly on every news station, as it was approved for hospital use. But what was it? Few people had heard of it, and even fewer even knew how to pronounce it.

This drug had been around for quite some time. Its primary use, however, was to help those with autoimmune diseases—like rheumatoid arthritis or lupus. While plenty of drugs get prescribed "off-label," that is, to help with conditions outside of those that they are approved to treat, this one was never officially approved by the FDA or CDC.

Although it's not an antiviral drug, it was found to at least be marginally helpful for those suffering from COVID. Its popularity surged throughout the hospitals, and people who contracted the disease were looking for a way to get the drug at home as well.

In the meantime, the IRS was clearing out all their facilities. Everyone was sent to work from home, but as we saw, that wasn't completely happening.

Dr. Anthony Fauci, the Chief Medical Advisor to the President, was on the news daily, explaining the latest about COVID and where the disease was going.

With somber words, he made it clear that our current level of social distancing and staying at home wasn't working as well as everyone had hoped. Without major steps taken, the current plan would still result in a death toll of more than two hundred thousand individuals.

Looking back, we can see that a death toll of two hundred thousand would have been a much better scenario. At the end of March, the official number of COVID deaths had barely reached a thousand across the entire USA. Things would get much worse before they even started to get better.

CHAPTER 29

FOR RENT

When we were wrapping up 2019, our firm had five offices in two states, and a couple of remote employees in two more states. These spaces were designed to maximize productivity for employees, depending on where they lived.

Four of these offices were in the San Francisco Bay Area—one was "virtual." When the Loma Prieta earthquake destroyed the office building in 1989, we transitioned from a gathering space where people worked daily to an office that really didn't have employees but was designed to accept incoming mail and book conferences for clients who were local to the area.

The second office in the Bay Area was fully staffed with a conference room of its own. The lease on this office was set to expire at the end of October 2020. The building owner gave a one-year notice (in 2019) that to renew the lease, the rent would essentially double.

The third office was similar to the first: a virtual office that could be used on an as-needed basis.

The fourth, similar to the second, was fully staffed and included a conference room.

The fifth office in Arizona was fully staffed, but there wasn't a client-facing conference room. No clients came to this building. The two remote employees lived in Virginia and Pennsylvania.

While having more offices isn't always a good thing, we found that over the years, it streamlined business and helped make it easier to meet with clients depending on where they lived. Rather than have them navigate difficult California traffic, they were able to meet in a more convenient location.

COVID shook things up (metaphorically, not the same way the Loma Prieta earthquake shook things up) and caused us to rethink our office layout.

In the first office, the virtual one, nothing changed. It was often closed, especially in the heart of the pandemic shutdowns.

The second office was vacated and sat unused during the COVID stay-at-home periods. After months of nobody working from this office, we seriously considered the costs associated with renewing our lease—details to come on our decision for this one.

The third office was closed during the stay-at-home periods, but then it was turned into a full-time office for one of our employees who was formerly in the second office and wasn't able to efficiently work from home.

The fourth office was vacant for several months, and then everyone returned when it was deemed safe to do so.

The fifth office, in Arizona, was vacant for a while. When restrictions lifted, some of the employees returned to working in the office, but the complex had started major renovations, making it difficult to concentrate. These renovations went on and on and lasted for well over a year.

One of our virtual employees retired, and we added two others by the time the dust settled and life was back to normal.

But throughout this period, it felt like musical chairs. When we decided to vacate office number two, we had to figure out how to move everything from a three-thousand-square-foot office space into storage. When few people are working, tracking down a moving company and renting storage units becomes quite the logistical nightmare. But in the long run, it sure beat spending thousands of dollars to rent a space where nobody would be working from.

Of course, as we tried to keep business running as (mostly) usual, we still had deliveries. We had to coordinate schedules so someone could be in the office when deliveries came in, but only one person to minimize contact and keep our gatherings under the ever-changing stay-at-home orders.

Cleaning crews were still working; they were essential. They had important jobs to sanitize everything to ensure germs from one day were not lingering when someone showed up the next. But not every employee wanted the cleaning crew in their office—we had to devise a way to ensure that some offices were cleaned regularly and others were left alone.

Then, there was the issue with clients. They would see cars parked in front of the office and assume we were back in business, despite the fact that the county health departments had said nobody was supposed to be operating in person. Signs on the doors stating that no clients were allowed inside were ignored, and it became a part-time job just telling people that we weren't seeing clients in person.

Our cups were already running over with more and more being poured in all the time. And we weren't even near the end of the pandemic.

SUMMARY OF SECTION III

The first few months of COVID were a roller coaster. Nobody knew what was going on, not even the experts. We were all told to sit tight and hang out at home, and within a couple of weeks—a month at the most—this virus would run its course and we could return to life as normal.

Congress, however, caused a lot of problems in the accounting world.

While they were the cause of the problems, they really didn't have much of a choice. Despite the bureaucracy and the mess they generally caused, I have to hand it to them. They did their best and pushed legislation through that normally would have taken years to get approved.

Throughout my forty-year career, I have experienced nothing but good, hard-working people at the IRS. They didn't get a say in what was happening—they just had to follow along with the new laws that Congress was pushing out on a daily basis.

Let's dive even further into that rabbit hole and see what problems were created for us.

IV

Day 75 – Day 89

CHAPTER 30

SUITE DREAMS

Travel and hospitality industries were tanking. Companies were watching stocks plummet with their profits. But people still had yet to cancel their travel plans. They were hoping that by the time May rolled around, things would be completely opened back up. The world wasn't in chaos, it was in limbo.

Travel companies were in a pickle, though. Often, hotel rooms, airfare, and the like were nonrefundable. They relied on those fares so they could keep things moving. But with the shutdowns, how would tourism-dependent businesses stay in business but not irk their clients and future clients?

Hotel rooms are, by nature, finite and perishable resources. If a room goes unsold, it can't be shelved for later use. It can't be stored and tapped into later. Every day those rooms aren't booked represents income that is lost forever.

But when there's uncertainty of what is coming, nobody wants to book a hotel room that they may not be able to use. If they even could book hotel rooms. Travel bans, mandatory shutdowns, and stay-at-home orders meant that few places were even allowing guests during this time. In the coming months, the situation would slowly begin to open back up, but even then, they opened at a diminished capacity.

Travel companies that operated cruise ships were some of the hardest hit. With social distancing not even an option, if one passenger got sick with COVID, it quickly spread to others on the cruise ship. But that's not the worst of it. If there was a COVID case on board, it was incredibly difficult to get passengers off the ship . . . even if they weren't sick.

With countries shutting down their ports, ships couldn't even dock to unload passengers if they tried. The CDC issued "no sail" orders, and quarantines meant that thousands of passengers were stuck aboard for not just days, not even weeks, but in many cases, over a month.

The biggest issue: Nobody had answers. They didn't know when they would be able to disembark.

CHAPTER 31

AWE AND DOMINATION

As the world shut down, I'll never forget the environmental impact of having fewer people going about their daily lives. In the bigger cities, the effects were much more profound.

China had some of the most restrictive COVID shutdowns. The air quality in places like Beijing showed just how big of an impact humans make on the environment. Within a matter of days, nitrous dioxide levels began to decline. Within a few weeks, levels had dropped by as much as 30 percent. This pollutant, found in high quantities in areas of heavy population, causes respiratory difficulty and can lead to acid rain. It turns out that the best way to reduce pollution may be to force people off the streets.

It wasn't just nitrous dioxide levels depleting, though. Visible pollution, such as the smog that heavily grips Southern California, was clearing up. You may even remember the videos of how the canals in Venice, Italy, went from a murky brown to nearly crystal clear. So clear that dolphins started swimming in them as their curiosity was able to be satisfied without the fear of encountering humans.

Areas throughout India were suddenly seen to be healing as people stopped interfering with nature. The Bay of Bengal began to clear, the Ganges River (Ganga) was once again drinkable as industrial dumping ceased. The sea water at Cox's Bazar Beach—the world's longest natural beach in the world—visibly changed color as people stopped swimming and boating there.

Even noise levels were suddenly all but muted. In Delhi, studies showed that noise dropped by 40 to 50 percent.

The world was able to pause and look around at how humans interact with nature. We could, in real time, see the damage that we were causing to the planet—and how the earth was able to heal itself when everyday lives stopped for just a little while. For years, debates have waged about how we can clean up the earth. Trillions of dollars have been spent trying to restore, clean, and fix the damage that we do to the planet. It turns out the best way to heal the planet is to stop messing it up in the first place.

Now the biggest questions regarding the environment that passed through most people's minds were, "Can we keep it this way? Will this be the kickstart we need to finally see that we need to reduce pollutants?"

Now, several years after the initial shutdowns, we can see that it didn't last. Our environmental harm is just as bad as it ever has been.

It didn't matter where you looked, life was affected by the novel coronavirus. Not only were all the news stations covering it twenty-four hours per day, but every aspect of our lives was affected by the virus. Since businesses were closed, or at least operating differently, we had to learn how to live with this new normal.

While the environment was healing itself, we changed how we lived.

Those living in senior facilities were stressed out and having a hard time with the lack of contact. But then, our grandparents learned how to use video calls.

Restaurants weren't allowed to have customers dining in, but they couldn't just close indefinitely. People were forced to eat at home, but being stuck at home doesn't mean you suddenly have the ability to prepare tasty meals. Uber Eats, DoorDash, and other food delivery services took off.

If it was deliverable, it was booming. Remember how the hospitality and cruise ship industries were being hit hard? From the beginning of March to the beginning of May 2020, Royal Caribbean Cruises saw their stock plummet by nearly 50 percent. Amazon, however, saw their stock rise by 30 percent over the same period.

Finances aside, people were dying. The US edged out Italy for the most COVID-related deaths—although nobody really knew how many people had died from the virus; there were many who died before they started keeping track. With the new record of the most deaths, the US government had to step up once again and try to mitigate what was going on.

Any time there's a contract awarded from the US government to a private company, procedures follow. Bids go out, they have to be analyzed, and the best option is chosen. During war or during national emergencies like a worldwide pandemic, the government can override those procedures to hasten the process.

They did this by passing the Defense Production Act. As people were dying, hospitals were filling up. COVID, a respiratory illness, affects breathing. Patients required ventilators to survive, but ventilators were in short order.

When the US government put out the call for a company to produce these machines in bulk, General Motors stepped up and said, "Yeah, we can make ventilators." This is an auto manufacturing company, a company that doesn't have a background making medical equipment. By the middle of April, they had secured a $489 million contract to produce thirty thousand ventilators before the summer was over.

Meanwhile, every time we turned on the TV, every time we hopped online, we were met with statistics showing an ever-increasing number of COVID cases and COVID deaths. This virus wasn't slowing down. It wasn't going to go away in a couple of weeks. It would, however, end up dominating the planet for years to come.

CHAPTER 32

A THOUSAND CUTS

COVID-related issues kept piling on.

If you ask your accountant about 2020 and 2021, they will likely tell you that these were the worst tax seasons of their lives. If you push a bit, you'll likely learn that the tax season that started in February 2020 really didn't end until April 2022.

Personally, I did not have a real day off during those 800 days. Not a single one. COVID impacted our industry severely both in the office and outside of it.

Don't get me wrong, I'm not minimizing the impact the disease had on others. The healthcare workers who put themselves in harm's way every single day, the first responders who saved countless lives, and the other essential workers who kept us from dying are all heroes. I wouldn't trade places with them. My intent, however, is to shed some light on what accountants went through as we were largely behind the scenes. But the disease impacted many people throughout our communities.

Accountants and tax preparers are helpers. We love solving problems for our clients, at least when it comes to the financial aspects of their lives. But when COVID-related accounting laws were changed on the fly, we typically didn't get paid anything extra to handle the influx of work. Often, that influx left us rather unfulfilled, as we didn't know the answers and couldn't solve the problems.

The dramatic changes to unemployment laws were a big issue.

Many accountants have little experience with unemployment benefits. Aside from going to the state's unemployment office and applying for benefits, we largely don't do anything with how those benefits work.

We do, however, know how they are taxed. And we know that our business clients must pay unemployment taxes, so if one of their employees files a claim, the states have something to fall back on. Now, as COVID had caused a shutdown of IRS hotlines and an overrunning of California's EDD (the unemployment offices), clients had nowhere to turn but to their accountants. We were, after all, the problem solvers and the "person who knows finances."

Our phones started ringing with unemployment questions.

"Do I qualify for unemployment?"

"How much unemployment benefit will I get?"

"How long will I be able to collect these checks?"

"I have not been working, but now I can't even look for work. Do I still qualify?"

"I heard that sole proprietors can claim unemployment now. Is that true?"

And perhaps the most amusing, because it's way outside of our realm of expertise, "Can you help me apply?"

We had few answers to those questions. Yes, people who had not been working and now couldn't look for work did qualify for benefits. Yes, sole proprietors and partners could claim unemployment (historically, they were not able to do so). But as for the rest of those questions? We were pretty much just as in the dark as everyone else.

Now, unemployment seems like it's rather straightforward. You apply, you get approved, the following year you receive a 1099 that shows what you collected, and you pay taxes on it. Of course, when the EDD issued several 1099s with incorrect amounts, clients came calling for the one person who knew taxes—their accountants.

Your accountant was already working extended tax season hours for months (my firm went to sixty-hour workweeks the day after the Super Bowl, and we stuck with it until Tax Day). Every time Congress announced a new change that affected money, our phones rang even louder.

Every one of those calls meant additional time, additional stress, and additional frustration that we had to deal with, often for free. Plus, we were still filling out tax returns.

CHAPTER 33

WHERE'S THE AUDI?

If you walked into someone's house, would you know how many cars they had? You could figure it out by peeking into the garage or counting the number of car keys in their possession. With Mark, however, nobody knew how many vehicles he had. To top it off, there was a missing vehicle that didn't even have a key to go with it.

Mark was back in the hospital, and only one friend or family member was allowed visitation at a time. His foray into living at his home again was short. With his rapidly declining health, there was just no way that he would have lasted on his own. I was still trying to deal with his finances, and we all hoped he would pull through.

I drove to his bank to try to figure out which accounts were which and get some sort of order going. Naturally, the doors were locked—nobody would let me in.

Estate planning and preparation is a time-consuming process to begin with. There are a ton of unknowns, and every one of them needs some sort of answer before you can move on to the next issue. With COVID locking doors, delaying services, and doing COVID things, this process was taking three or four times as long as usual.

I went to his brokerage firm to try to figure out Mark's investment accounts. The same issue. Doors were locked, but I could see people moving around inside. Banking and investments are considered essential, and this stuff had to get done. Eventually, someone saw me standing at the door and cautiously opened it.

When I explained who I was and why I needed to talk to someone about Mark's estate, I learned, "We are only meeting with regular customers, and by appointment only."

They didn't know me. I wasn't getting in.

On the way home, I stopped at the grocery store. Eating out wasn't an option; some delivery was, but many people, including us, were buying food and preparing it at home. That meant more customers shopping and shelves wiped cleaner than usual. Shopping meant putting on your mask, going one direction down the aisles, staying six feet apart, and then not even being able to find the product you need. And that meant another shopping trip the next day. Just buying the essentials meant a couple of trips and a much longer process than usual.

Efficiency was tossed out the window. Banking couldn't do customer service. Governments were shut down. Even something as simple as a death certificate took weeks to acquire—and you couldn't do any estate planning without a death certificate.

Mark kept great records of his assets. But even with those great records, it took *forever* to get a grasp on how to handle his estate when his inevitable passing finally came.

CHAPTER 34

AIRBORNE?

At first, we were told that masks wouldn't do a whole lot to stop the spread of the virus.

But then, we were told they would help.

Soon, it came out that a mask would help but it had to be an N95 mask.

Eventually, we were told that cloth masks were better than no masks.

Neck gaiters were an easy option, quick to pull up and cover the face . . . but then they weren't a good option because the particulates could pass right through.

With all the information being fed to us at a rapid-fire pace, many people had no clue what to believe, who to trust, and when the information would change. To top it all off, it was getting harder and harder to trust the WHO.

The US government was acting quickly. There was no way anything would get passed and changed if laws weren't fast-tracked.

We saw it daily, and while it created problems for the accountants, it had to be done.

The WHO, on the other hand, didn't seem to change their procedures. They weren't keeping up with real-time processes. As Congress took every shortcut imaginable to fast-track the changes, the WHO moseyed their way through traditional bureaucratic methods. It was as though they were merely going through the motions because that's what they had always gone through.

It's no wonder that frustrations with this organization were on the rise.

The World Health Organization was way behind and seemed to be stumbling along when the announcement came out that the COVID virus could be transmitted via the air. Headlines read, "The Coronavirus Can Be Airborne Indoors, W.H.O. Says." They went on to explain that people can carry the virus and be asymptomatic, two disclosures that many experts believe should have been announced much sooner than they were.

The WHO's processes slowed down the release of information so much that they were way behind the game when they finally announced it.

CHAPTER 35

OPEN SHUT, OPEN SHUT

Just about everyone wanted to get back to work. Having the country shut down had huge impacts across the board, and returning to business as usual was, obviously, the goal.

That impact was even more profound on organizations that simply could not work remotely. Organizations such as the IRS.

We were all told to shelter-in-place and work from home if possible. Unless, of course, you were an essential worker. But what was essential? Nearly anyone could claim they were essential and not have to worry about following the orders.

Despite all that, people were trying to work from home, essentially homeschool their kids, manage a house, and deal with the rest of the chaos the world had fallen into.

The IRS was forced into a pretty bad spot.

In the middle of March, thousands of IRS employees were told they had to work from home. But they didn't have training on how to do that, many likely didn't have any office space at their homes, and even if they did have space, they simply didn't have the right office equipment to get their work done effectively. Throw all that into the mix that these families were now all home and going stir crazy, and it's no wonder they shut down, then opened quickly, then shut down, then opened . . .

By the end of March, most IRS employees were working from home—or at least attempting to do so.

By late April, guidelines were released on how the IRS, and other federal agencies, would be able to return to the office and get back to work at least in a somewhat normal capacity. By the time May 2020 rolled around, nobody knew if they were coming or going; they couldn't decide if they would recall employees, send them back home, or come up with some new plan.

I believe that the IRS was destined to fail that tax season. They simply had no other options.

1. Their workforce was trying to work from home, but they didn't have the resources.
2. The pandemic struck at the worst time of the year for the IRS.
3. The increased workload from COVID-related legislation—such as the issuing of stimulus checks—created an unreasonable added burden.

By the time employees were filtering back into their offices in early May, the IRS had tens of millions of unopened pieces of mail. To put that into perspective, if you opened one piece of mail every second, around the clock, it would still take you twenty days to open every letter.

They could never catch up.

CHAPTER 36

APRIL 15

Remember back to your college days and the feeling that washed over you as you finished your final exam for the year and you were "free" for the summer? For accountants and tax preparers, that feeling is every April 16 . . . the day after Tax Day.

Except in 2020.

Tax Day had been pushed out three months. So, when the middle of April came, nobody celebrated, nobody hung the "Closed" sign on the office door, and nobody hopped a plane for a well-deserved vacation. Instead, it would be another three months before we could even consider those things—at least, that's what we thought.

On the surface, however, moving the tax filing deadline out three months looked pretty simple. Just delay when things are due, right?

Sure, for those simple returns that just needed a 1040. But a lot more tax-related issues are due on April 15 in addition to yearly filing. What about a corporation trying to file their annual taxes after an extension put their deadline in the middle of April?

Were quarterly deadlines extending? What about funding a previous year's IRA? Payroll taxes, sales tax returns, and estimates—we never really got answers to when all of these were actually due in 2020.

Tax Day 2020, for me, had much bigger implications. I received a call that Mark had passed away the night before while in the hospital. Not only did I lose a great client, but as the executor of his estate, I had to figure out how to tie up all the loose ends. This would have been difficult enough during a normal year; this year, it was frustrating beyond belief.

Before we could even get started, I had to drive fifty minutes north of my house to Mark's—it would be even longer if there was traffic, but nearly everyone was staying home. I then spent hours and hours going through his belongings to locate his records. Fortunately, he was meticulous with his records, but it still took a lot of time to figure out what had value and what didn't.

Only then could I look for an estate sale company to help liquidate the assets. A feat that turned out to be next to impossible. There were particular rules regarding estate sales, and the bulk of the companies offering this service wouldn't even consider this project.

Meanwhile, I was on the phone with the funeral home to set up a memorial service for Mark. Arranging the time, I asked, "When can I come by with one of his suits so you can dress him?"

Their answer, "Oh, no, sir. We can't allow anyone in the building, nor can we accept outside clothing or belongings. When the time comes for the service, we will be limited to ten guests in addition to the clergy. If more than ten guests show up, we have to immediately end the event."

I still had to find a Realtor who would list (and show) the property. I was working on getting leftover estate sale items to Goodwill or another thrift store that was taking donations. I had to track down titles to vehicles (likely in the safe deposit box at the bank . . . which I was unable to access) and let anyone else with ties to the household know that Mark had passed.

For instance, the gardener. As I searched through the household records, I discovered checks were paid to what appeared to be a gardener. After placing a few calls to what was listed as the contact number—and never hearing back from them—I gave up.

As I said before, everything was taking at least three times as long due to closures and working from home.

And that's not even including the timeshares that Mark and his wife owned. They had several in Hawaii; some of them were really nice. In an era when travel was restricted, and small islands like Hawaii were some of the most restricted, how do you sell a timeshare without drastically cutting the price?

Normally, Tax Day is a day of celebration and relaxation. This year, it was loaded with more hours of work than there are in a day.

SUMMARY OF SECTION IV

Life became different. We saw that when people stopped polluting, the Earth started to heal quickly . . . Later, we learned that we could mess things up rather quickly too.

Our daily lives changed. The way we lived life changed. And for those who work in accounting and the tax preparation industries, we were absolutely overwhelmed with how much was coming at us on a daily basis.

In fact, it was faster than daily—changes were coming at us almost every other minute.

Governments could hardly decide what to do. Around the country, every state, even every local government, was handling things differently. The federal government had another idea of what was best, and they decided to push Tax Day out three months—extending the hardest tax season of my life by (what I thought) three months. It turned out to be much longer than that.

V

Day 90 - Day 151

CHAPTER 37

WELCOME TO A NEW REALITY

Historically, changing laws took a long time. As topics were hotly debated, passed back and forth, argued over, and ultimately agreed on, we could follow along to get a feel for where they were headed.

It could normally take a decade to change a major law, like those that apply to estate taxes. Even when the law is passed, it can get tied up in the court system for months or years before we know how to interpret it.

Take all those systems, all those processes, and all those checks and balances, and throw them right out the window in 2020. That year, the process looked like this:

- Congress passes a law
- President signs off on the law
- Law goes into effect
- IRS issues guidance (no time for debate, this is the best guess as to what it means)
- Nobody knows what to do

Sounds complicated, right? Now do that several times every single day. Many of the laws had to do with finances and taxes—keeping the economy alive was a huge priority. Other laws related to other areas of life. Many had to do with funding to keep organizations alive until situations could get back to normal . . . an idea that was becoming increasingly distanced and obscure.

Up and down the line, everyone was impacted. The DMV, restaurants, grocery stores, you name it. Health departments had constantly changing rules, hand sanitizer became a staple on everyone's shopping list, and touchless products (think automatic doors, sinks, and soap dispensers) surged in popularity.

To top it all off, there was no consistency between departments. Police forces had varied codes from city to city; states had to come up with their own rules; fire, military, and healthcare all interpreted the shutdown differently.

Meanwhile, somebody—or more likely, a group of people—was thinking up new regulations, writing them down, and implementing them. All this before anyone was even caught up with the other new regulations that had just changed the day before.

Three years later, we're back to "normal" government operations. Every new law has to be budget-neutral (this is why we have sunset clauses on laws: to keep them within budget parameters). Those parameters weren't around back in 2020, and for a couple of years now, Congress has been dealing with the fallout that continues to occur from laws that were passed without due diligence being done.

Of course, we didn't have time for due diligence; people had to survive.

CHAPTER 38

WHAT? NO RMDS?

IRAs, that is, Individual Retirement Accounts, are popular retirement investment vehicles. If you retire from a job that offers a 401(k), you can roll that 401(k) balance into your IRA so you have complete control over it (no need to go through a previous employer anymore).

Before 2019, you had to take a Required Minimum Distribution (RMD) every year starting on the year you turned seventy and a half years old. This RMD was calculated based on the balance of your account and how many years you had left to live based on average life expectancies. If you failed to take your RMD, you were hit with a penalty of 50 percent of the amount you didn't withdraw (this could end up being tens of thousands of dollars).

In 2019, before anyone even heard of the novel coronavirus, Congress passed the SECURE Act (the Setting Every Community Up for Retirement Enhancement Act of 2019). This new law stated that if you reach seventy and a half in 2020 or later, you could delay your first RMD until April 1 of the year that you reach seventy-two.

Sticking with me here? Because things are about to go on a wild ride.

Nearly everyone dislikes RMDs. If you needed the money, you were already taking withdrawals from your IRA; if you didn't need the money, you were forced to withdraw and then pay taxes on it.

This new law changed when you had to take those RMDs, but nothing else—they still used the same algorithm and they still forced clients to withdraw even if they didn't want to do so. Except by the time it went into effect, the CARES Act had passed. And part of the stipulations in the CARES Act were that you didn't have to take RMDs in 2020—the goal was to make sure people weren't withdrawing money when the market was at the bottom. Wonderful! Like an answer to prayer . . . right?

We had several hundred clients who took RMDs. As soon as it was announced that they were waived for the year, our phones started ringing.

Immediately, issues were coming up.

- Will California follow this same rule?
- Will other states follow the rule?
- What if I already withdrew (you have sixty days to reinvest the money)?
- What if I withdrew in January, and the sixty days are past?
- What if I had taxes withheld? Will the IRS put those taxes back?

As the phones kept ringing, we kept thinking, "Surely the Congress and the IRS will fix these issues."

Eventually, they did. But it wasn't until June 23 when the IRS announced that you had until August 31 to put the money back—at that point, it was three weeks until Tax Day and just a few weeks after that to contact all of our older clients to let them know that they could put their RMDs back.

Despite these new stipulations, problems weren't solved.

Suppose you withdrew $100,000 from your IRA. $30,000 was automatically withheld for taxes, and you received $70,000. But you didn't need the money, and since RMDs were waived, you opted to put it back in.

You couldn't return $70,000 and ask the IRS to return the other portion; you had to put $100,000 back into the IRA. That meant digging into other sources of income, savings, or selling assets to come up with that chunk of money.

The $30,000 paid in taxes wasn't just gone, though. It was rolled over as a payment toward the next year's tax liability. Okay, that sounds reasonable.

Except that in 2020, your income was $100,000 less than in most years. So, your tax rate could be changed, and when 2021 came around and you filed taxes for the 2020 year, you could have overpaid . . . a situation that re-presented itself in 2022, when your income had returned to normal and you were underpaying.

Accountants everywhere recognized that this would be a huge problem. But with every problem, there is opportunity. That temporary bump into a lower tax bracket allowed for Roth conversions—a Roth IRA does not have the required minimum distributions that a traditional IRA has, and this conversion alleviated a lot of strife going forward.

If it were only that easy, because now I was on the phone with even more clients, telling them that if we converted to a Roth, they could set themselves up for a better tax situation in years to come.

And that meant more hours of work when there were already not enough hours in a day.

CHAPTER 39

INTROVERT'S DREAM

I'm an introvert. In fact, many of those in the accounting profession are introverted by nature. We love to crunch numbers, we meet with clients as necessary, but as you know, those interactions can be draining—exhausting, sometimes.

As COVID shut things down, there were suddenly fewer people in places where there were often a lot of people. Even the roadways were far clearer than ever before. Not that we were really driving anywhere.

Winter had faded away, and spring was bringing about green grasses, blooming flowers, and warm sunshine during a time when beaches, golf courses, and other areas of outdoor recreation would normally be buzzing with activity. Instead, in 2020, they were all but deserted; veritable ghost towns. With the daytime temperatures peaking in the seventies, it wasn't hot, and it wasn't cold. With diminished traffic, pollution was at an all-time low. It seemed that Mother Nature even wanted us to get out and enjoy the fresh air, as I don't remember any rain during this time (think: drought).

There was no need to get dressed up for work—we weren't going into the office anyway. There was no commute, the few meetings we had were via Zoom, and there were no after-work social obligations, no networking events, and no weekend barbeques. In other words, it was the introvert's dream. Without the need to make excuses for not going to that social gathering, we were able to recharge.

We live near a large golf course. But nobody could get out there to play golf, so the only people around were the grounds crews as they maintained the greens, trimmed bushes, and managed flower beds. Instead of a long commute in bumper-to-bumper traffic, I was able to get up at sunrise and enjoy a long walk through the course without upsetting golfers.

Now, it wasn't all sunshine and butterflies. With the new laws being passed, managing Mark's estate, and the overall tax season burden, I was working sixteen-hour days, seven days a week. But these walks (where I would often be on the phone making sure everything was getting done) helped maintain my sanity. In fact, I have no doubt that if I were still trying to commute and handle office affairs, I wouldn't have made it through this period.

The world, however, is largely made up of extroverts. As my fellow introverts and I were recharging and loving the peace and quiet, the extroverts were chomping their nails, wondering when this thing would be over so they could get out there and socialize.

Despite this silver lining, we can all agree that very little good came from the pandemic. Even though morning walks through the golf course were nice, I would give them all up in a heartbeat to be able to visit my dad, who was living in an assisted living facility at the time. I believe just about everyone would do so as well. A little more time with loved ones is worth far more than the introvert's dream of peace and quiet.

CHAPTER 40

PAYROLL PROTECTION PROGRAM— THE PPP

The purpose of the PPP was to save jobs—it did that. And I tip my hat to Congress and all of the government employees who worked tirelessly to implement programs like these during COVID. This is what the government can do when they need to act quickly.

Many successful companies could have survived the pandemic without these loans. However, they would have done so by sacrificing the very jobs they had created. It's just a good business decision to protect the company during uncertain times by laying off workers. Despite the negative publicity that some big companies received by taking the PPP loans, that's what they were for. Congress basically said to them, "Keep your employees; we will subsidize you." It worked, but it did cost a lot of money.

It also cost accountants a lot of time. The PPP loans were all that anyone talked about for a long time.

Nearly all of the big banks came on board and offered these forgivable loans as the economy was being stimulated. Soon, smaller community banks joined in as well. As the PPP popularity grew, every client who owned a business wanted to jump on board. But because the legislation was passed so quickly, very little guidance was offered about how to use these loans the right way.

Loan amounts were based on an eight-week average for payroll. But what eight weeks do you use? Can you use the eight weeks that included massive bonuses? Or does it have to be regular pay periods?

Then comes the question of what happens when you take the loan but later lay people off? What if you use part of the loan for payroll, but it's still not enough?

How do you keep records to show that you kept people on payroll? And what if you hire new employees—can you apply for more PPP money?

This program started out with $660 billion in funding and was just one of many different government programs designed to keep the economy functioning optimally while nothing was functioning optimally.

Accountants around the country, known for their meticulous recordkeeping, were tasked with figuring out how much their clients were able to apply for and then justify that the loan was used appropriately so it could be forgiven at a (largely) unknown later date.

For my own firm, we weren't struggling, but we didn't have the influx of cash that usually comes with tax season. When the deadline was moved out three months, it also meant that income was stretched out over three months as well. So, do we apply for our own firm, even though it was possible that year-over-year, nothing would really change?

We were still preparing taxes. We were still thinking that COVID would clear out by the time summer came (no more of this two-week nonsense, as that time came and without any fanfare). Toilet paper and hand sanitizer were still the hottest commodities around.

Life was just a blur.

CHAPTER 41

DEVIL IN THE DETAILS

There was so much uncertainty around the PPP loans that it wasn't even funny. And since the accountants are in charge of tracking finances for companies, we had the fun job of trying to add certainty to an uncertain time.

Throughout April, a month when we are usually finishing up tax returns and then jetting off on a much-needed vacation, we were fielding phone calls about the PPP loans. Nearly all of them were the same questions everyone else had: Do I qualify? Do I have to pay it back? Does it count as income? How does this affect the debt on my balance sheet?

Our best answer: Document everything. Then document even more.

Because the questions like "Do I qualify?" were the easy ones to answer. But peppered into every conversation were more difficult questions. Ones that did not have answers right away. For instance:

How do I actually measure wages?

Do employee tips count as wages?

Can nonprofits qualify for this loan?

What if ownership changes before the forgiveness or payback period?

How do I even get forgiveness?

Do healthcare benefits count as wages?

What is a full-time equivalent?

What can I do with the money?

And on, and on, and on.

This wasn't the only program going on at this time, either. The Employer Injury and Disaster Loans (EIDL) needed to be dealt with, the Employer Retention Credit (ERC) had to be learned, and then there was a program called the Payroll Tax Deferment. We'll get more into that in a later chapter—we just recommended a straight "no" across the board if anyone asked if it was a good idea to look into this one, but every phone call just added to the time spent talking to clients about their specific situations.

It wasn't just that every day, there was a new program to learn about. It was that every day, there were several new programs to learn about—many from the federal government and many from the state governments. If you are an accountant who works with clients from multiple states, you have to stay on top of the details from all the programs, from all the states . . . most of which you just have to give your best guess on how to deal with them, and expect to fix the problems later.

BLUR

Everything was happening so fast. Life was moving quickly but standing still at the same time. We were in tax season, clients were panicking, we were trying to keep everyone calm, but life and work were a big blur.

As people were working remotely, kids were home and had to be largely homeschooled.

When we did go out, it was to a series of stores, looking for the right supplies. My route included grocery stores, big box stores, office supply stores, and home improvement stores. I would put on my mask and start at the store where I knew I could get most of my provisions. But every time I went to Costco, the toilet paper aisle was bare. I would make a note and move on to the next store. Hand sanitizer was out at that one, so I would check the next one. It was often a three- or four-stop trip to gather up the essentials of daily living.

We were still being told that this would all be done in "two more weeks." Of course, after two weeks, it was still "two more weeks." As distrust grew, supply runs became a little more frantic. When an item was actually in stock, we bought extras because we didn't know when it would be back in stock again. That created even more shortages.

Tax Day, the original Tax Day, anyway, came and went. Nobody had gone anywhere for well over a month, and nobody knew when we would be able to get back out there. Should we even bother planning a vacation? Tax season was still nearly three months away, so we couldn't even think of a vacation until then.

As an employer, we were dealing with requests from employees. Since we had an extra three months until Tax Day, could they take a mini "vacation"? That "vacation" was to go see grandkids or family. Those requests came more frequently in a frantic, yet somehow unfrantic, world as we were in a bit of a holding pattern.

Life under quarantine moved at such a slow pace, with bursts of activity, that everything was a blur. So many needs were vying for our attention, and none of them could get our attention. Most of the country was just trying to survive, get through the pandemic, and hopefully get back to life as usual without the weird distractions.

CHAPTER 43

HOW MUCH IS A TRILLION?

Our minds are not set up to grasp some of these large numbers and concepts. As finite humans, we might live to see one hundred years old. So, to comprehend a million years, or even a billion years, takes serious contemplation.

After the Coronavirus Aid, Relief, and Economic Security Act (CARES Act) was signed into law on March 27, 2020, there was an influx of $2.2 trillion into the economy. It seemed that this was really the first time "trillion" worked its way into most of our lives.

But, because we don't deal with such numbers, it's hard to comprehend how much money this is. We can try to put it into perspective in a variety of ways. Let's look at it simply from a money standpoint.

Suppose you wanted to repay this $2.2 trillion loan at a rate of $1,000 per day. How long would it take to repay the loan?

2.2 trillion divided by 1,000 equals 2.2 billion days.

2.2 billion divided by 365 (days per year) equals just over 6 million years!

Even if you bumped your repayment plan up to $1 million per day, you'd still be on the hook to repay this loan for over 6,027 years.

We're still dealing with numbers that most people can barely grasp—what's the difference between $1,000 per day and $1,000,000 per day? Very few people could afford any of that.

Suppose you wanted to count to 2.2 trillion. How long would that take? If you could count one number every three seconds (yeah, you can go faster, but consider how long it takes to say 1,047,991,122), you'd be counting for a long time.

2.2 trillion times 3 (seconds) equals 6.6 trillion seconds.

6.6 trillion divided by 60 (seconds per minute) equals 110 billion minutes.

110 billion divided by 60 (minutes per hour) equals 1.83 billion hours.

1.83 billion divided by 24 (hours per day) equals 76.38 million days.

76.38 million divided by 365 (days per year) equals 209,000 years.

Again, what if you wanted to take a 2.2 trillion step hike? How far would you travel? Suppose one step equals 2 feet in length.

2.2 trillion times 2 (feet) equals 4.4 trillion feet.

4.4 trillion divided by 5,280 (feet per mile) equals 833 million miles.

833 million divided by 24,792 (miles around the earth) equals 33,612 laps around the earth.

One last one here. Suppose you took a football field and wanted it covered in 2.2 trillion dollar bills.

It would take 517,000 bills to cover the entire field. You would have to cover the field 4.255 million times.

Each dollar bill is .0043 inches thick, meaning you would have a stack of bills 18,297 inches, or a total height of 1,523 feet.

Suffice to say, we're talking about a lot of money here.

The US government is notorious for "fake" accounting—they cook the books tremendously. So bad, in fact, that the AICPA testified to show what it would look like if the government had to account the same way that a publicly traded company had to account.

Now the big question was: Where would all this money come from? In fiscal year 2022, the government brought in a little over $5 trillion; this bill alone was nearly half the money brought in during a given year—and keep in mind that reduced economic activity in 2020 and 2021 meant the government brought in far less than that.

How will this bill be paid for? Where is the "extra" $2.2 trillion coming from?

CHAPTER 44

JUST THE FAQS

So much legislation was coming out of DC without clarity that someone had to step up and make sense of it all. Since the PPP was backed by the Small Business Administration (SBA), they decided to issue some clarifying statements and put out an FAQ page that would help businesses and accountants figure all this out.

What happened, however, was that they further added to the confusion.

Remember, the goal of the PPP loans was to provide certainty in an uncertain time. Instead of laying people off to ensure there were no major hits to the business, the loans let businesses keep people employed—and the loans would be forgiven if certain requirements were met.

The FAQs from the SBA, however, told a much different story. There were rules on necessity, stipulations on a company's liquidity, and more. All of which raised more questions than they answered, but then there was Question 31: "Do businesses owned by large companies with adequate sources of liquidity to support the business's operations qualify for a PPP loan?"

It's a great question, but the answer muddled things up a bit. It claimed, "Any borrower that applied for a PPP loan prior to the issuance of this guidance and repays the loan in full by May 7, 2020, will be deemed by SBA to have made the required certification in good faith."

Based on this, we heard that anyone could apply for the loan. But wait a minute, oops, if you had enough liquid capital that you didn't really need the loan, you could repay it by May 7 without any questions asked.

May 7 was ten days after the FAQs were first available. Ten days to contact every single business client, go through a checklist of whether or not they *really* needed the loan, and then repay it so there were no penalties, late fees, and interests, or just to be considered as a no harm, no foul.

There was an uproar among the US accountants—this was just not feasible. So the SBA, thinking quickly, pushed the deadline back another week. Businesses then had until May 14. Again, not really feasible, and the uproar was still loud.

Congress jumped in at that point. Now they were clarifying that if you needed help, or you were uncertain whether you needed help, this loan was for you. Without those months of back-and-forth, this couldn't get clarified before pressing "GO!" and it was left to the SBA to interpret the rules . . . in this case, that interpretation happened incorrectly.

Boil it all down to this: Accountants were hearing from every business owner client that read Question 31 and was concerned that they had made a mistake by applying for this loan. And now they were worried that they wouldn't get it repaid in time . . . then what would happen? Would their business credit be shot? Would the business be flagged?

In the end, the misinformation wasn't a game-changer; it wasn't a big deal. But we all spent that week with our heads spinning before we realized the FAQs had the wrong information, and it added hours upon hours of phone calls that all resulted in, "You're fine, keep people employed, the loan will be forgiven if you meet the criteria."

CHAPTER 45

SANITIZE

Anew reality was settling into the world. People were buying things they had never purchased before and hoarding items that were as common as . . . well . . . toilet paper. New terms were being thrown around to encourage people to stay six feet apart.

We were all trying to create a safe living environment. The experts told us that the virus struggled to travel through the air more than five or six feet, so "social distancing" entered our vocabulary. Signs popped up everywhere, encouraging us to "stay six feet apart" or, in the rest of the world, "stay two meters apart." When it was discovered that people didn't know how far six feet was, grocery stores would add "two shopping carts apart."

Hand sanitizer had been commercially available to the US public since the 1980s. But suddenly, it was on every shopping list, yet on none of the store shelves. As soon as the shipment arrived, eager shoppers snatched up every last bottle.

Big cities became eerily silent as most residents stayed put. Some, however, ventured out of the crowded cities and moved back home with parents in smaller towns or rural areas where fewer people meant less likelihood of being exposed.

It was, however, more frustrating than anything.

Three years from that point, after the world began to open back up, I was on a trip to Italy. We were at a popular honeymoon spot and bumped into a couple from Atlanta—they were honeymooning long after their actual wedding had taken place. In 2020, they had only recently started dating, and the young man decided to introduce his girlfriend to his parents. A weekend trip to the lake house at the beginning of the shutdowns turned into what could have been a nightmare: the two were stuck there for months, waiting and wondering what would happen.

My own children had their travel interrupted as well. My daughter lives in Thailand with her husband. When they came to visit in early 2020, they couldn't make it back home to Thailand when international travel was closed for all non-citizens. They were "stuck" at home with my wife and me as we all navigated this new reality together.

Clorox wipes became the staple for center consoles; we wiped down the steering wheel before and after driving anywhere. If we went into the office, we wiped down the desk, the chairs, and the doorknobs. We went from washing our hands a couple of times every day to ten times every day.

Truck drivers were shipping toilet paper as quickly as it rolled off the shelves. Why haul a heavy load when you can get paid the same to ship toilet paper—a commodity that was so scarce that stores limited sales to one package per customer.

It was commonplace to have a mask in your pocket, another in your car, and extras hanging with the car keys. You didn't go anywhere without it. And nobody really knew what kind of mask they should get. N95s were the gold standard, but suddenly the market was flooded with fake N95s. But did it matter? Some masks were homemade; some were merely neck gaiters.

Walking into a store wearing a mask pre-COVID meant a robbery was about to take place. Not wearing a mask during COVID meant danger.

The world was suddenly sanitized, and we all were trying to keep our closets stocked with cleaning supplies.

CHAPTER 46

WARP SPEED

April 30, 2020—Operation Warp Speed was announced. The goal of this effort was to fast-track the vaccine, to take a process that usually took several years and make it happen in several months. If the fast-tracked legislation was an example of what could be done at warp speed, then this vaccine should be able to be developed at warp speed as well.

This endeavor was bigger than Apollo 11—the first manned mission to the moon.

In 1969, NASA was in the middle of the Apollo missions. By this point, a number of successful space missions had been completed, and now there was a race among the countries to see who could successfully land on the moon first. With a budget of $355 million, Apollo 11 wasn't just expensive, it was a feat for humankind. It wasn't long before that space travel was a pipe dream, and now we were talking about sending people not only to space but to disembark on the moon. It was huge!

Operation Warp Speed was even bigger, and not just in terms of money. At a cost of $11 billion, the thought was that if we threw a whole bunch of money at this project, it would make it go really fast. Which, to an extent, is true. More money for research and development means more human-hours on the project and ultimately faster progress.

Among the scientific community, however, a whole lot of skepticism existed. It just didn't seem scientifically possible to create the vaccine and test it to ensure not only efficacy but also safety.

$11 billion emerged from somewhere, and the vaccine development was underway.

Beam me up to somewhere, Scotty, just get me outta here!

CHAPTER 47

ECONOMIC IMPACT

Economies can only stay healthy when people are spending money. It has to keep moving. In times of uncertainty, however, people tend to stop spending and start hoarding. Especially when most businesses were shut down—we couldn't go to the mall, we couldn't go out to eat, and we couldn't spend on entertainment.

So, the government came up with a plan to give away a whole bunch of free money. Each time, it was still under the idea that COVID would be over soon and we just needed a little boost to keep the economy moving forward.

Stimulus packages were announced. These stimuli came in rounds: the first one was $1,200 per adult and $500 per dependent. Later, those amounts would increase to $1,400 per person—adult or dependent.

Initiating and distributing an economic stimulus is not easy. It requires much planning, work, and follow-through. But the announcement was made first, and then Congress had to figure out who got to determine eligibility, how the money would be distributed, and all of those details. The logical organization that already dealt with money was their choice, and the added workload fell to the IRS.

This huge organization, already working remotely without the proper training and equipment, and in the middle of tax season, was now supposed to handle this huge project. They weren't even properly staffed to handle day-to-day operations, and now Congress wanted them to handle an economic stimulus?

There were, naturally, rules that went along with eligibility. If your income was over the limit ($75,000 for single filers; $150,000 for couples filing jointly), then no stimulus for you. To determine what your income was, the IRS looked at tax returns. For those who had already filed their taxes for 2019, those numbers were used; for those who had not yet filed, they would look at the 2018 returns.

Who do you think had the opportunity to explain the stimulus regulations to all of their clients? Yep, the accountants.

We were absolutely inundated with calls. Many of them merely repeated the same questions, and we were answering as best we could.

For example, a married couple was claiming their twenty-two-year-old as a dependent . . . even though that child was out on their own. The couple received the $500 "bonus," and the adult child received nothing. Is there a way to file an amended return to get the child off so they get the full amount? The answer was, "Yes, but it's going to cost more than it's worth."

There were clients who had already filed their 2019 returns, and they were just above the threshold: no stimulus for them.

They were calling to ask if they could "un-file" so the 2018 return could be used and they would qualify. The answer was, "No, you can't un-file for any reason."

Some clients were in the middle of filing their 2019 returns, and they knew they would be over the threshold. So we were asked to wait to file their return until after the checks came in.

But that led to the question of whether they would have to repay the stimulus if they ended up being over the eligibility threshold.

And of course, the question on every client's mind was: "Is this taxable?"

Eventually, Congress came out with the answer to that one, "No, federal taxes will not be owed on this stimulus." State taxes, however, were another story. Every state had to decide that for itself and whether or not it would be taxing those amounts.

And the calls just kept coming.

"When am I going to get my check?"

"Will it be direct deposited?"

"Where will they send the money?"

"I closed my bank account; will I get a check instead?"

"I have moved; will the check be forwarded?"

Accountants were trying to survive the busiest and most hectic tax season of their lives. Now call after call came in, asking questions that didn't have answers. We had to put forth our best guesses and say, "In this situation, here is how I would handle it."

Call, after call, after call . . . and that was just for the first round of stimulus payments. Ultimately, there would be three of them—causing tax headaches for years to come.

CHAPTER 48

FUNERAL FOR A FRIEND

Mark had a lot of friends. Some were in California, but many of them were from different areas around the country. They came into his life at various times, like the friends he made who lived in Oregon and were part of his circle while he was attending optometry school.

With all these friendship groups, many of the friends didn't know each other. They all had known Mark and his wife, but they didn't know each other. This put me in an awkward position when it came time to arrange his funeral.

As I mentioned, the funeral home would only allow ten guests, plus the clergy. Any more than that, and the service would be immediately terminated. That, however, wasn't the only strange rule we had to abide by.

Services were only allowed to last for thirty minutes. Friends and family were not allowed to carry the casket, so no pallbearers would be around. When the service was over, everyone had to disband right away—nobody could stick around as the casket was lowered into the ground or the dirt was placed back into the hole. To top it all off, it was standing room only. No chairs, no seating, and stand six feet apart.

Working with a couple of Mark's closest friends here in California, we came up with a list of ten people who would want to come pay their respects. We opted for a closed casket funeral, as we couldn't get him dressed up anyway. I decided to let another friend attend the funeral while I waited in my car, watching the service from a hundred feet away.

As I contemplated what a pain it was to go through someone's final memorial like this, I was quickly reminded that even with the restrictions, we weren't so bad off.

It was during this same time that hundreds of pine box caskets were being lowered into mass graves on Hart Island off the coast of the Bronx in New York City. This island, with a long history of being a public cemetery, was inundated with burials. Hundreds, and eventually thousands, of individuals (many of whom died from COVID) were being gently placed into long trenches. No funeral, no memorial, not even a headstone acknowledging their existence—just burying the bodies of those who didn't survive the pandemic.

My irritation washed away as I realized that this was no fun but so many more here in our own country (not to mention those who passed in countries around the world where even a pine box funeral was too much to ask for) didn't even get the luxury of a simple, hastened, standing-room-only funeral.

CHAPTER 49

BLACK SWAN EVENT

COVID was an unprecedented event. It spurred many other unprecedented events. These black swans will make sense in the coming years when we can fully analyze what exactly happened and fully understand the true impact it had on society, the economy, and the environment.

But early on, we didn't know what to do. And the government did what they needed to do so the US didn't just collapse. Part of that was to issue PPP loans so businesses could keep going. We talked about how those affected those of us in the accounting world, but the magnitude of the PPP numbers is what makes the situation unique.

After major disasters, low-interest loans are available to help businesses recover. For instance, after Hurricane Katrina devastated the Gulf Coast, over four hundred thousand loans were issued for a total of $10 billion. That was a massive undertaking and one that helped those in New Orleans and the surrounding areas recover when otherwise they would have been unable to do so.

Just a couple of months after COVID emerged on everyone's radar, and just a few weeks after the country shut down to prevent the spread of the virus, PPP loans were available. In less than a month, more than four million loans were issued and over $500 billion was distributed.

Remember a few chapters back when we talked about how big the CARES Act was? $500 billion is no small number; in fact, an individual could spend $10 million *per day* for over 130 years and still have money left over.

Money was rapidly flowing through the government at this time. Money that was almost just "up for grabs" with little oversight on who was getting what, when it would be repaid, how it would be repaid, or even if it would be repaid.

Throughout the world, similar programs were taking place. The European Union put together a plan called NextGenerationEU—a program that was designed to help European countries come out of the pandemic not only still operating but better and thriving. With a budget of over €800 billion, it was one of many programs designed to provide a huge influx of cash so economies didn't collapse.

Other programs, localized to states in the US or countries around the world, were doing the same thing. Throw money at the problem and hope it doesn't get bigger.

And it worked, but it came with a whole lot of collateral damage.

TOWN HALLS

Across the country, accountants were confused and overwhelmed. There were so many changes and so many new laws, with so little clarification, that we were all left scratching our heads and trying to figure these things out.

Apparently, the American Institute of CPAs was in the same boat. To set the collective accounting minds at ease, they launched a weekly town hall webinar. Originally, it was designed as a short-term solution to provide answers when there really were no answers. However, it has continued—although episodes were slowed to every other week—and recently aired their one-hundredth episode.

These town halls were an absolute lifesaver. They were one of the only reasons I kept my sanity. I wasn't alone, either. Episodes aired at lunch time, and I was joined by over ten thousand other participants to try to figure out what these new laws were all about. Now, instead of banging my head against the wall alone,

I knew I was banging my head against the wall with thousands of other frustrated accountants.

One episode contained substantial information about FAQ 31.

Businesses that had already obtained a PPP loan were worried that they would have to pay it back. However, this town hall helped to clarify that Congress's intent wasn't for recipients to repay the loan—the intent was to keep people employed. In fact, it was determined that Congress didn't want a business to repay the loan; if they had to repay it, that meant they laid off employees.

While there wasn't a black-and-white answer, many of the town hall meetings would result in the idea that "This is the most likely situation, and this is what you should do."

Regarding the PPP loans, the answer was document, document, document. Fortunately, accountants are already pretty good at keeping detailed records.

I cannot stress enough how amazing these town hall webinars were. Whoever was working behind the scenes on them figured out just what accountants needed to know, and every week, they did all the research necessary to put forth information we were wondering about. It must have been hours and hours of research every week to condense it all into a one-hour-long webinar that, in my opinion, saved many people from leaving the accounting profession completely.

CHAPTER 51

MY OWN BLACK SWAN

It was a couple of months into the pandemic, and we were settling into a new reality with a new routine. Essentially, my routine was to wake up, eat breakfast, and then walk thirty feet to the office. Eat lunch, then work. Eat dinner, then work. Sleep. Repeat.

A few times each week, I would drive to Mark's house and take care of any issues that were going on over there. Upon returning home, it was a quick shower to disinfect after being out and about.

There came a point when I realized that this time wasn't going to end soon. We had to settle in for the long haul despite the claims that it would all be over in a couple of weeks. I didn't want to look back at life under quarantine and realize that I didn't make the most of the time spent.

Hindsight, of course, is 20/20—anyone who was watching the stock market could have made a fortune with all the adjustments going on. Of course, you could have lost a fortune too!

But it wasn't all about making money from the pandemic; maximizing the situation could mean a number of different things. For instance, suppose you went to prison. Would you wallow in pity, or make the most of the time by reading books and developing yourself personally?

Over the course of the first year after things shut down, I made it a habit to take my solitary walks through the golf course. I felt it was a great way to relax and clear my head. Meanwhile, I would listen to TED Talks and podcasts to increase my knowledge. A fringe benefit was that I lost over forty pounds—it helped that restaurants were closed down so we were forced to eat healthy meals at home.

Every change in our reality presented another opportunity if we would take the time to capitalize on it.

Nobody was going into the office anymore: Was there a way to maximize that situation?

Supply chain issues kept coming up: Did that create an opportunity?

As mentioned, the stock market was moving: Could those movements be captured for gain?

About two months into the pandemic, I started to see some of these opportunities, but I wasn't entirely sure what they meant. Besides that, we were still in tax season. I was still handling Mark's estate, and with all the new laws and changes, I hardly had time to sit and think—let alone figure out how to capitalize on some of these big opportunities.

CHAPTER 52

FOUR MILLION LOANS—$500 BILLION

Again, I have to take my hat off to the government and the Small Business Association for taking action so quickly. Thinking up the PPP loans and planning them was a feat in itself. But then they were organized, administered, and followed up on within days.

Within weeks, millions of loans were processed, and hundreds of billions of dollars were distributed. All without clear guidance or clear answers on who was eligible, what would be forgiven, or even how to determine the amount a business could apply for.

These loans created more questions and answers.

Then, as we saw with FAQ 31, the answers created more questions. Which led to the answers being changed—they just had to; otherwise, the program would fail. The changing answers led to more questions. It was a constantly moving target. Every change just dripped a little more workload into the already overfilled lives of accountants (and certainly those working in many other industries as well).

Accountants and payroll staff were supposed to record and document everything, but when the requirements are constantly in a state of flux, how do you know what to keep track of? How do you even keep up?

What started out as an "eight-week rule"—one that stated the money had to be spent within eight weeks—changed to a twenty-four-week rule. Of course, there were questions about employee retention. What if you had a full staff when you applied, but then workers voluntarily quit before you received the loan?

There were changes regarding who qualified: Could a sole proprietor with no employees obtain the loan?

What was a qualified expenditure?

How were the loans forgiven, who did you talk to, and who actually forgave those things?

For that matter, when would it be forgiven? Would recipients have to pay interest on the loan until some date that hadn't even been set yet?

Completely new forms were necessary just to keep track of and process these loans.

The SBA was overloaded with work, so someone at the AICPA (American Institute of Certified Public Accountants) finally took matters into their own hands. They drafted up the forms with as much information as they could possibly see as necessary to document every detail that had to go along with these loans, and sent them over to the SBA.

Even with the release of new forms, that didn't mean that the calls and questions from clients would stop or even slow down. No, they meant that now we had a nice list of all the questions that clients would be asking . . . still without solid answers as to what it all even meant.

IS THIS INCOME?

Some of the questions on the loans had at least reasonable answers. Maybe we didn't have the official word, but we could make our best guess as to what would be the most likely scenario.

As the loans were flooding in, businesses around the country were collecting money. But this influx of cash raised a whole bunch more questions.

One of the biggest questions was, "If forgiven, will this money be counted as income?"

The PPP loans were started in May, but we didn't have an official answer from the federal government until September of that year. We finally heard, "No. PPP money will not be counted as income on your federal tax returns." Great news for those who received the loans, but still insufficient advice. What about state taxes?

Furthermore, there were many other factors to consider when applying for a loan, collecting that loan money, and having it hang out on the books. Most businesses couldn't just ignore the fact that they had this outstanding loan because they felt it would be forgiven at some arbitrary date in the (hopefully) near future.

They still had to abide by the loan covenants established with their bank. For those small businesses out there that maintained a line of credit, they had certain conditions they must maintain in order to keep that line of credit. When they took out this PPP loan, they went outside the boundaries of those covenants, and now they were considered to be non-compliant.

For instance, suppose you were a small business that had $400,000 in debt and a $100,000 line of credit that you needed for operating expenses. In the covenants, the bank issuing that line of credit may have included a line item that said your credit would be inaccessible if your entire debt exceeded $500,000. If you received $100,001 in PPP loans, your debt was now over the threshold.

But there was still a big issue that few had anticipated. It had to do with the basis adjustment for the loan that was forgiven (even though it was non-taxable at a federal level).

S corps pass through everything to their shareholders. If your S corp makes $100,000, it is reported on a K1 and taken out as a distribution. At the end of the year, your corporate tax return would show $X in profit, and $X went out to shareholders: no gain, no loss.

But now there was money that came in from the PPP loan. It wasn't money that came in as income because it's not taxable and it wasn't technically income. But the business that made $100,000 then showed that $125,000 came in (income, plus a $25,000 loan). How did they account for that extra $25,000?

The only way to balance the books was for the PPP loan to be coded as income so that at the end of the year, $125,000 came in and $125,000 went out. Suddenly, this non-taxable loan appears to be taxable because distributions exceed the basis—even though Congress said it wouldn't be taxable!

A program that was designed to help keep people employed flooded accountants' inboxes and voicemails around the country. For months, even years, to come, it became an accounting nightmare that had little guidance and few answers.

More drops into an already overflowing cup of tasks and priorities.

CHAPTER 54

HOW LONG WILL THIS TAKE?

Pre-pandemic, obtaining a death certificate wasn't a terribly difficult process. If you requested one on Monday, you would usually have it by the end of the week; if they were backed up, it could take seven or eight days. Now, however, death certificates were taking three times as long.

Government officials were working from home. So you couldn't take the required paperwork down to the courthouse to apply for the death certificate. Instead, you had to scan and email it and hope it found its way to the right person.

But even getting the right paperwork was cumbersome. Hospitals were inundated with COVID patients. Deaths were skyrocketing to the point where mobile morgues were set up in tents in the hospital parking lots. It took extra time to get the information from the hospital over to the county clerk, and then even more time to get the death certificate from the clerk.

Estate administration can't move forward without a death certificate.

I had been over to his house numerous times doing some house cleaning. I was busy tracking down valuables, figuring out what they were worth, and making calls to locksmiths, estate liquidators, appraisers, and realtors. Of course, I had to tell them that the death certificate was not in hand, so it could be another week . . . or another month. Nobody actually knew. Finally, weeks after Mark's passing, I had the death certificate in hand and I was able to move forward on wrapping up his estate.

Mark's friends and neighbors knew he had passed, and suddenly, there was a whole lot of interest in Mark's house. This house, located within walking distance of the Google campus, was in great shape and in a great location. People were coming out of the woodwork, asking to see it because they thought they could score a great deal on it. Property values were depressed, after all, and since it was an estate closeout, things should move quickly (read as: low cost), right?

That created an even bigger dilemma for me. I wasn't working with a Realtor yet, so if someone wanted to see the house, I had to drive an hour there, show the house for an hour to a stranger who might have COVID, and then drive an hour home. It was three hours out of my day to receive a low-ball offer and risk being infected.

When I finally tracked down a good estimate on what the house was worth, I explained to those calling that even if we saved Realtor fees, the house would still be over $2 million. Most, if not all, were shut down when they realized they weren't going to get a screaming deal on this property.

Slowly, things started getting settled. But there was still Mark's art, jewelry, and cars that needed to be appraised (when no appraisers were available), bank accounts that needed to be closed (when banks weren't taking appointments), and the rest of the goods that needed to be donated (when thrift stores weren't accepting any items).

It was a series of calls, emails, and phone tags that added steady drips into the already overflowing workweek.

CHAPTER 55

FORGIVENESS AND COMPLIANCE

Everyone who received the PPP loan was assuming that it would be forgiven. Few would have applied if the rules for forgiveness were too difficult to meet.

The question on everyone's minds at this point was, "What do you have to do to have this thing forgiven?"

Companies receiving this money were worried about dotting the i's and crossing the t's. Accountants were worried about recordkeeping so that when the audit came, did they really qualify? Little doubt was in anyone's mind that these loans would be audited—the government doesn't just hand out hundreds of billions of dollars and hope for the best.

How do you make sure to account for all the loan money? How do you make sure that nothing is mixed up in such a way that your forgiveness can be negated?

My firm developed a plan that we recommended to every business client that would help them keep their records straight. As soon as they received the PPP money, they should move it into a separate bank account. It was so much easier to show where the money went when it was not commingled with other funds.

Then, shortly before each payday, transfer out just enough to cover the qualified payroll expenses. This way, when the audit did come, it was easy to show exactly where the money went. This minimized the chances of the auditor saying, "This money is commingled; it's too hard to trace."

Of course, we were just guessing. Everyone was just guessing.

As the loans were being planned, there was talk (for a short while) that before any loan would go out, the application and forgiveness requests would have to be certified by a CPA. In the accounting world, there was a collective hard blinking, a sigh, and a "What?!" Who was supposed to sign off on this? Who even qualified to be able to sign off on it? What about CPAs who don't go through peer review? Could they certify it? Ultimately, this was dropped as quickly as it had come up; CPAs didn't have to sign anything.

More and more questions were popping up. How were full-time equivalents (FTEs) determined?

If you used the PPP loan money to buy supplies, were those costs still deductible for tax purposes?

Congress wrote the law that said the PPP loans were available. The president signed it into action. It was determined that the SBA would work closely with the Treasury to monitor and administer the program. The SBA scratched its head and came out with some rules and regulations, such as FAQ 31, which we mentioned turned into an absolute debacle. Congress jumped in and said, "Woah, wait a second. That's not what the intent was!" And eventually, these new laws that were hastily passed had to be re-legislated to clarify what the intent really was.

That re-legislation, however, came well after the fact. Long after the loans were distributed. Long after they were forgiven (or, in very rare cases, repaid). Long after taxes were finalized, the laws came out that said, "Hey, remember several years ago when we had those PPP loans? Yeah, these are the rules and regulations you were supposed to have followed."

CHAPTER 56

THEY GOT HOW MUCH?

Because the PPP loans were government-funded, information about the companies receiving them was considered to be public domain. When the press found out about that, they tracked down those who received the biggest payouts and posted a whole bunch of stories about them.

For instance, the LA Lakers received $4.6 million . . . which left a lot of people scratching their heads and wondering why we were giving a basketball team millions of dollars. To be fair, whoever was in charge of the Lakers did later decide to repay the loan so other businesses with greater needs could be helped.

The same can't be said for a lot of other big-name companies, though. Dozens of businesses received the maximum $10 million payout. In fact, 1 percent of the companies receiving loans took in 25 percent of the entire "pot" of PPP money.

It was a gold mine for the presses, a concern for business owners, and further nightmare fuel for accountants.

If all this information really was public information, who would be looking it up? A business client now was wondering if they would be scrutinized by the IRS and also by the public. What about those businesses that didn't really need the money, had a booming business, but still qualified? Would they have a PR headache on their hands?

Guess who fielded the phone calls and questions about what was going on? It certainly wasn't the IRS (remember, their client-facing phone numbers were shut down), and the SBA was up to their necks processing loans.

The purpose of this program was to keep people employed. It was not based on need or financial ability to keep employees. It was to keep people employed . . . that simple. Keep them employed, don't lay them off, and we'll provide the funds.

For the accountants, though, it was critical to document what the "thinking" was when clients signed the PPP application forms. What was happening in their business? In their industry? With their supply lines? With their employees? We were often the ones who needed to do the work of documenting.

For the public, it didn't matter. For those who didn't own the business, all they needed to know was that the paychecks would keep coming. And that's exactly what the PPP loans did. It is estimated that this program saved fifty million jobs.

If you do the math, that comes out to $10,000 per job saved. Did the program have a huge economic impact? It certainly did. But would the impact of fifty million jobs lost be greater than $10,000 per job? Most likely, it would.

Ultimately, accountants were still trying to keep up with the added workload. And many of us were uncomfortable charging our clients extra for this. When they asked questions, it was just part of the job. So call after call, email after email, and text after text just added to our workload.

CHAPTER 57

ART, JEWELS, COMPUTERS

When you walk into someone's house, you quickly notice things they have. You'll notice the décor and the artwork on the wall. If you're discerning, you can tell whether it's a nice painting or a printed replica.

Most of us, however, won't be able to tell an original masterpiece from a painted reproduction. It could be a million-dollar Picasso hanging over the mantel, or a knock-off that cost a couple hundred dollars at a swap meet.

As I took inventory of Mark's house, I had no idea which paintings were worth a fortune (if any), which were worth just a little, and which were worthless. The same goes for jewelry—his wife had jewelry, but without a professional opinion, it could have all been cheap costume jewelry, for all I knew. And as I found out, appraisers were hard to come by.

It would have been much easier to just post everything for sale and take whatever offers came rolling in. However, as Mark's accountant, I had to act in a fiduciary capacity. That meant being diligent in managing the estate and making sure I wasn't selling artwork for a few hundred dollars when it was valued at tens of thousands of dollars.

I discovered that Mark had a few computers in the house. All of them locked down with passwords. I knew there was a way to access a computer without knowing the password and methods of accessing the data by "hacking" into the machine. But I had no idea where to start.

I spent hours searching the house and going through filing cabinets and ultimately found a list of passwords—some of them allowed me access to the computer. The other passwords helped me get into his various online accounts.

It took a lot of time searching the house to find the notebook with a list of passwords. Once I was able to access the computer, I could find valuations and copies of receipts for most of the high-value items in the house. Ultimately, discovering the notebook saved far more time than if I had gone through item by item and searched online for the value.

CHAPTER 58

POLARIZED

The US, and the world in general, has been highly polarized for a long time. There are so many different worldviews, so many different ways of living, and so many different philosophies of life that it's amazing we can all agree on anything to begin with.

By the time May rolled around, we started to see even more polarization in our own country.

Those leaning to the right were saying COVID was overblown and we could ignore it. Those leaning to the left were all behind Fauci and the lockdowns. Some were saying it was a conspiracy, others were saying it was made in a lab, some said we had to do all we could to protect the vulnerable, and others said every number was fudged anyway and the vulnerable would be just fine.

Vaccinations had become a hot topic, and they weren't even available yet. Compound the issue with rumors abounding that the Moderna vaccine, one of the most popular vaccines in the US, was being developed by a company backed by Bill Gates, and suddenly, a significant number of people believed we are going to be implanted with microchips.

By May 5, the Trump administration began to dissolve the coronavirus task force. But then they reversed that decision, and the task force continued.

On May 11, France began to ease restrictions—half the population thought that was a good idea, and the other half thought it was insane.

On May 29, the US announced that the country would formally withdraw from the World Health Organization.

Religious gatherings had been halted, but wasn't there a separation of church and state? Why was the government allowed to say people couldn't gather together to worship?

Shouldn't we have just let this thing run its course and flatten the curve that way? Should we really have been so cautious about a virus that was "essentially just the flu"? On the other hand, couldn't we flatten the curve by "starving" the virus? Lock everyone down so nothing could spread? Was the virus really "just the flu"?

There was a lot of information being thrown at us daily. Some of it was true, some of it was false, and everyone latched on to the information that best fit their worldview—those who believed something else turned into bad guys.

We were already polarized. This became yet another topic to fight about.

CHAPTER 59

NEW ACCOUNTING TERMS

COVID didn't just create more work for me and accountants across the country. COVID created entirely new accounting terminology; the whole way we did business was upset by the legislation that was rapidly being pushed through Congress. Suddenly, we were faced with terms that we didn't have a clue what they meant, and we had to quickly learn how to define them.

Those definitions literally changed by the minute—as soon as one idea was defined, it was being revised.

Now, we're talking about:

- FTE Reduction Quotient on a Schedule A
- Safe Harbors for Expenditures
- Restoration of Salary/Pay Reduction
- Covered Period
- Alternative Payroll Covered Period
- Loan Forgiveness Calculators
- The Payroll Protection Program Flexibility Act

Every time we figured out the answer to one question, three more questions stepped in to fill its place. There was close to $1 trillion out there through various loan programs (not just the PPP), and nobody knew if any of it had to be paid back. Or what the rules were regarding having the loan forgiven.

For instance, if you had a business that received $250,000 and the government said, "Just follow the rules, and you don't have to pay it back!" But you wondered, "What are the rules?"

One of the early rules said that you had to use 90 percent of the amount you received on payroll expenses within eight weeks. But it didn't clarify when those eight weeks started. Was it when you received the loan? Was it when you first tapped into the loan? Was it some arbitrary start date in the future? Could you pick and choose your eight weeks and align them with payroll periods?

Of course, there is always the question of whether the business closes . . . is the loan still forgiven? If an employee quits, do you have to repay the portion of the loan that you were planning to use on their salary? What about a terminated employee, an employee who passed away, an employee who was out for most of the eight-week period because they were sick with COVID? Without clarification, every accountant had to just give it their best guess until we were well into the trenches.

The Payroll Protection Program Flexibility Act came out in early June and provided some clarification (and most importantly, flexibility) so that accountants everywhere could stop banging their heads against the walls. But there were still plenty of questions and plenty of work to be done to make sure business clients were set up properly and wouldn't be dinged later.

SUMMARY OF SECTION V

Over the course of 2020, more laws were passed that affected people's taxes than I have ever seen. Since they were passed so quickly, questions abounded on what they actually meant, what we should do about them, and how to handle them in particular circumstances.

We saw tax deadlines extended, unemployment benefits increased, PPP loans, stimulus programs, and new acts that cost trillions of dollars. We also saw opinions becoming increasingly divergent—some were intensely concerned, while others were not concerned at all.

Every one of these changes created challenges for those who deal with taxes. They created questions without answers and piled on the hours of work that we had to do.

VI

Day 152 – Day 800+

CHAPTER 60

HOW IT SHOULD WORK

When I first started my career as an accountant, I was employed at one of the "big eight" accounting firms. To this day, I believe this experience was the most valuable part of helping me get to where I am now. Anyone who wants to become an accountant should absolutely work under other accountants as they get their feet wet.

Working for this firm, we were all expected to keep up with pending tax legislation. In earlier chapters, I described how that happens: a lot of back-and-forth until things are finally resolved and ready to go. However, when it's pending, there are so many questions and so many unanswered items that it's almost not worth the time you spend reading. It does, however, make for some wonderful bedtime reading—it will put you to sleep in no time.

Later on in my career, I simply did not have the time to do this, nor was it expected by the clients of our smaller firm. The most efficient use of my time was to wait for all the legislative changes to be made, regulations to be released, and continuing education to be developed, and then invest the time in learning the new laws that had been passed. This would typically be months after legislation was signed. Hopefully by this time, there was guidance from states as to how they would treat the federal law change.

The amount of new legislation in March and April of 2020 was beyond comprehension. We were expected to get our arms around it as it happened. This was a completely new world for our profession.

The government is usually convoluted and burdened, but what they did during COVID was amazing. Everything went so quickly; it was truly incredible. The only problem was now they had to clarify all these new laws that were signed onto the books and implemented—what was their intent, and did we do it right?

To top it all off, any time there's legislation out there with billions of dollars of "free" money, there will be a whole lot of fraud. The PPP program issued four million loans. How much money do you think was handed out to fake companies? How about companies that fudged their numbers? How do you even keep track of all that, and how do you track down those fake companies? By the time anyone can go back and audit these things, the fraudsters will be long gone.

CHAPTER 61

FIFTY MILLION

The PPP loans helped stave off economic collapse, but there was still a lot of fallout from COVID. Even as people were staying employed, hundreds of thousands were contracting the virus daily and the death toll continued to climb—there was no flattening the curve.

Even with fifty million jobs saved, unemployment was skyrocketing. As more and more people were laid off, the official unemployment rate ticked up from 3.5 percent in February to 13 percent just three months later, a rate that hadn't been seen since the 1930s when the US was going through the Great Depression. Most economists, however, agree that 13 percent is vastly understated, with the official number of those losing their jobs coming in much higher.

Hydroxychloroquine, the "miracle drug" that was thought to be highly effective at treating COVID, was "proven" to be ineffective for treating COVID. Yet just a week later, President Trump announced that he had been officially diagnosed with the virus and was taking hydroxychloroquine to help treat the symptoms—further adding to that polarization we just talked about among our already-polarized country.

Major sporting events were canceled. Some, like Wimbledon, had been going strong for over a hundred years—now to be rescheduled for 2021, assuming life would be back to normal by then.

Travel bans were in place around the world, with some countries, like Chile, issuing "immunity cards." If you had recovered from COVID, some thought that you were now immune to the virus. These cards showed that you were sick and recovered, and thus you shouldn't be able to be infected (or transmit the disease) anymore. Shortly after that, the WHO announced there was no evidence that recovered patients were immune. The world realized that in the coming months when patients were infected numerous times (often with the same strain, not a variant).

By the end of May, the US recorded over a hundred thousand COVID-related deaths, and the World Bank took a guess at the worldwide economic impact this virus would have.

The World Bank warned about impending poverty due to the coronavirus. Their claim: sixty million people would be pushed into poverty. Of course, how could you measure this? How could you even tell? Those were just best guesses based on the impact the virus had had after just a few months. These were the marginalized groups already. They didn't have access to services, healthcare, or even clean drinking water.

Here in the US, we don't see poverty in the same way that the world sees poverty. Millions of people aren't living paycheck to paycheck, because they don't get paychecks. They're teetering on the brink of nothingness. This estimate from the World Bank shows that those who were just clinging on would be forced to let go.

Remember, by the end of May 2020, many believed it would just be a couple more months and life would get back to normal. However, many more were beginning to doubt that—nobody really knew how long it would take for the world to recover.

CHAPTER 62

NOT SO FAST

By the time summer 2020 rolled around, most people realized that COVID wasn't going away anytime soon. All talk of "flatten the curve" and "just two more weeks" had vanished. People realized they weren't going back to the office for quite a while.

The reality was settling in. There wouldn't be summer vacations. There wouldn't be holiday parties. This thing would likely still be around when summer faded into fall, and winter settled in.

Shortly before COVID turned everything upside down, the lease for our three-thousand-square-foot office space in Palo Alto was up for renewal. Negotiations had begun, but the company that owned the building was literally doubling the rates. We weren't even close to an agreement when COVID forced everyone out of the office anyway.

For the next few months, we stalled. We had no desire to pay the increased rate on our rental agreement, and since COVID was putting a lot of decisions in a holding pattern, we decided it was best to see how things would play out. Why pay for an expensive office when we weren't even going into the office?

When summer came around and it appeared that COVID wasn't going anywhere, we reopened the negotiations. Our final offer: "We're out." We closed down that location since all employees were working from home anyway, and it was evident that we would be working from home for at least several more months.

That decision turned into a whole bunch of work. We still needed a physical space—one that gave us a mailing address, offered a place for clients to drop off paperwork, and provided accommodations for the handful of employees who occasionally needed a physical office space. Similar to a co-working space, the new office wasn't exactly an office—more of a place where we could hold client conferences (when it was safe to do so) and a holding space for mail.

All the furniture from our large office needed to be moved to storage, sold, or given away.

Now we were committed. There was no office to go back to even if things did magically open up. While the summer got going, we were working on finishing tax returns for the delayed Tax Day. Then, our continuing professional education and our company party (you know, the one we decided not to plan way back in February) would both be done virtually over Zoom.

Meanwhile, over in Arizona, our offices there were undergoing major renovations. The company that owned the office complex took advantage of the fact that everyone had cleared out and decided to do a whole bunch of updates when nobody was around.

Arizona, as a state, lifted restrictions far sooner than California did. These renovations, which were supposed to be done during

COVID closures, ended up taking two years to be completed—likely due to COVID restrictions and supply line interruptions. As our employees moved back to working from their offices, they soon found themselves forced back home because there was so much noise going on in the building.

Even when the desire to get back to work was there, employees were forced to work from home—such is the irony.

CHAPTER 63

SOFT TARGETS

In the beginning, we heard stories of this new virus that was making its way out of China into the rest of the world. Viruses start spreading quite often, actually, but usually they're shut down pretty quickly. Not many are as contagious as the novel coronavirus.

Then, the virus spread across Europe, and people became concerned. It eventually entered the US and became "real" to those of us who live here. Soon, it was all about tracing: if you were infected, you were asked to trace where you had been, trace who you had been in contact with, and try to follow it back so we could stop it before it got too far.

Finally, when tracing wasn't accurate, the news was flooded with stats. How many new cases? How many deaths? Who was being hit the hardest?

I'm sure these stories and reports captivated a lot of attention, at first. But as viewers and readers started to drop off, the media needed something new. Something fresh. Something that would bring the attention back and earn those views and clicks. What better way to do that than with human-interest pieces?

As COVID dragged on longer than expected (but nowhere near the actual end), the focus was on what were determined to be "soft targets." These weren't those who were infected or passed away from the virus; these were stories about the collateral damage that occurred because of the disruption to our day-to-day lives.

In the summer of 2020, I hadn't had a haircut for months. It was one of the shaggiest I had been since the 1970s. There were no hair salons open, and as much as I love my wife, I don't trust her with the clippers. How does a barber or hairdresser work remotely? They don't. And when they're closed for too long, they close forever.

Stores and restaurants shuttered their doors, never to open them again.

High school students eventually graduated after finishing their senior year online. They had previously planned to attend college, but why try to jump into a new era of your life when you can't even visit the campus? Spoiler alert: The next school year wasn't any better. The graduating class of 2021 even boasted about barely doing any homework but still graduating.

Elective surgeries were being postponed. Not that there was space at the hospital to accommodate anyone. Dental checkups were skipped. Many people even opted out of cancer checkups and screenings—and cancer rates dropped. Why? Because when you aren't diagnosed, it isn't reported. Fewer reports mean rates, on paper, drop. After COVID, however, cancer rates shot up dramatically.

First responders were overwhelmed. Many suffered from mental health problems because of the burnout.

And that's just in the US. Around the world, especially in countries where there weren't the services we had here, things got bad quickly. The number of orphaned children climbed as parents were lost to the virus. Even food and healthcare couldn't be administered to those directly or indirectly affected because charities were either shut down or trying to work remotely.

The world would have been in chaos—had anyone ventured out to do anything. But we were locked down, just trying to survive.

CHAPTER 64

KEEP ON KEEPING ON ... BUT ...

Around the world, different governments were trying to get life back to normal as quickly as possible. India started to open up a bit, the UK did too, and New York eased some restrictions. Other governments, however, weren't as quick to reopen. Some increased restrictions. Still others used this as a way to move their political agenda forward.

On July 2, India said they would start to reopen the country. There was controversy, as the country wasn't seeing a decrease in the number of cases—in fact, just a week earlier, they had been at an all-time high.

The next day, the UK opened travel again. Travel had been restricted from fifty countries around the world; those restrictions were removed.

In the US, the governor of Georgia announced on July 16 that masks were no longer required. Local government mandates were in place requiring people to wear masks in public spaces. However, the state's governor announced that the state's guidelines would take precedence. While masks were still encouraged, they were no longer required.

As the summer drew to a close, the White House resumed tours to the public after stopping them for the previous six months. These tours were, albeit, at a diminished capacity. Only 18 percent of the previous capacity was allowed in.

Also in September, Hong Kong began to relax social distancing measures. Dine-in establishments were reopened (with distanced seating), and fitness centers, spas, and businesses in the entertainment industry were allowed to open back up.

Despite the relaxed measures in many places, many more tightened things up. Some countries were opting for very restrictive lockdowns.

On July 4, the city of Melbourne, Australia, imposed hard lockdowns on a number of city blocks, including nine public housing towers. The lockdown was imposed after a spike in cases was confirmed, and restrictions were designed to minimize an outbreak.

That same day, in Spain, the entire province of Lleida was locked down as cases began to spread—more than two hundred thousand people were affected.

California closed indoor operations for restaurants, bars, and other dining facilities in six more of the counties. Kenya closed schools for the remainder of the year, and Washington, DC, imposed a new mask mandate (just days after Georgia lifted theirs).

By the end of the summer, New Zealand had locked down, Korea went virtual for over two thousand schools, and Finland had imposed curfews.

And, of course, many countries saw this as an opportunity to spread their propaganda and move their own agendas forward.

In July, France launched an investigation of their former prime minister to see if he had handled COVID properly. President Trump told Congress and the UN that the US would officially withdraw from the World Health Organization. The US, Britain, and Canada claimed that Russian hackers were targeting coronavirus research facilities . . . and then a few days later, the US accused China of doing the same thing.

By August, Russia had developed and approved the first COVID vaccine in an effort to be at the forefront of winning the war against the virus. This push for Sputnik V, however, was met with worldwide condemnation due to safety concerns. Their rush to be the fastest, the best, and the first meant they sped up the vaccine development and only tested on seventy-six individuals—far less than the many thousands necessary to determine how the vaccine would truly affect people. Nearly a year later, just 14 percent of the population had been vaccinated, in part due to the distrust of a Russian-made shot.

By the end of the summer, COVID was ravishing the world for over half a year already. And most populations were still largely clueless about what was going on or what we should do.

CHAPTER 65

NOT SO FAST ... AGAIN

Tax Day (July 15) came and went. Accountants everywhere breathed a sigh of relief. We figured that we had gotten through the bulk of it—the government couldn't possibly throw more at us, could they? Our cup was overflowing, but at least the drips didn't seem to be coming as quickly anymore.

Until August 10 rolled around. There was an executive order that payroll taxes could be deferred.

Now we were digging in to find out the true intent behind this law. What would happen? Who would it affect? How would it affect those who chose to participate?

As soon as this order was announced, the calls started coming in. The biggest question on everyone's mind: "You mean I don't have to pay FICA taxes?" If the answer was "correct," then that would be amazing—a big boon to employees and employers. However, that's not what the payroll tax deferral actually meant. This order said that employers could hold off on paying those taxes (for a short while). This meant that employees would have a temporary increase of 7 percent in their paychecks, and employers would have a temporary decrease of expenses by 7 percent.

But it was all temporary. Those taxes weren't suspended; they were merely deferred.

Not only was there such little benefit, but it raised a ton of questions that simply had no answers.

What if the employee quit, was fired, got laid off, or died? How would the taxes be repaid later? At the expense of the employer?

It was like a mini-stimulus now (more money in the check means more money to spend), but later, when checks are not just back to normal, but they're decreased by 7 percent to repay the deferment, what happens to the economy then?

Fortunately, this was at the employer's discretion—they could choose to participate or not.

Every client who called in asking if they should go ahead and do it was advised not to do it. We didn't just advise this; we highly recommended against participating in the deferment. We couldn't stress it enough; it was absolutely inadvisable to even consider it. Just ignore it and continue on with business in the new normal.

To our relief, none of our clients participated, as the headaches would have only been compounded. However, the calls and questions turned into a big fiasco—one more way to suck away any time we had.

CHAPTER 66

BLACK GOLD

In the early 1900s, Texas and Oklahoma were known for their oil fields. It was here that the term "black gold" was first introduced. But it really became popular in the 1960s when the TV show "The Beverly Hillbillies" aired. Oil has been a moneymaker for a long time, and for Mark, it had been a big source of his income.

Mark had inherited fifty-one working oil and gas interests. Located in Texas, they had been a wonderful source of retirement income. The only problem now was that with most things shut down, people weren't driving anywhere. Without motor vehicle traffic, oil refineries were operating at a reduced capacity, and without refineries buying oil . . . well, you get it. The value of crude oil was low. So low that it actually traded at a negative value—yep, the equivalent of paying someone to take it off your hands.

When the value of oil is so low, the value of the oil wells is little more than what the equipment is worth.

And that's where things get complicated. I work in accounting. I don't even dabble in oil and gas. I can crunch the numbers from the income those wells produce, but when you start throwing around jargon used in the petroleum industry, well, I'm either at a loss or trying to learn an entirely new language.

This whole new world of petroleum had a whole lot of nuances that I didn't even know existed. When I was tasked to sell fifty-one oil wells, I wondered, "Where do you even start?"

Because oil and gas interests are treated as real estate, the information on who owns them is considered public. Mark routinely would receive offers to buy the interests from him, and now I was receiving those solicitations. Of course, I was struggling to keep my head above water just to understand what these things meant!

Over time, I would get offers, and I would call the companies to find out more details. Little by little, I learned what the offers were and whether they were competitive, and I was able to find out which was legit and which seemed "off."

One day, an offer came in that was a bit ahead of the others. It was a higher offer from a company that knew they could sit on these interests for a year and then make a lot more money off them than what they paid for them. I did my due diligence, and they handled the rest of the transaction.

When the check cleared, I breathed a sigh of relief. In this case, to sell oil and gas interests, all you have to do is wait until someone who wants it more than you do comes along.

CHAPTER 67

SAYONARA SCHENGEN

When the UK decided to leave the EU, this Brexit disrupted many lives. Travel in that area once didn't require visas, but no longer would people have that freedom of travel. Those with an EU passport could go back and forth, with no time limits and very few restrictions, to any other EU country. No longer part of the EU, the UK didn't have that luxury.

As the fall of 2020 rolled around, it looked like much of Europe would go into a forced "Brexit." Governments were trying to return to a sense of normalcy, but as soon as things started to open back up, they were forced to close down again as a new wave of infections swept through the nations. It was one step forward and two steps backward.

Many were surprised as Hungary closed its borders. A member of the EU, this Schengen country (the Schengen Area is made up of twenty-seven European countries with "open borders" and no need for a visa to travel in or around these nations) was the first to close up the borders for all non-Hungarian residents. Was this a sign of things to come? Would this set a precedent that Europe would tighten up and be less open for intra-European travel?

One of the biggest problems was that nobody really knew how accurate these COVID cases and death numbers even were. People were certainly infected, and many people were certainly dying from the disease. But how many? Numbers, it appeared, were just WAGS—Wild Ass Guesses.

In the US, it was an issue. People were still dying from other causes, cancers, terminal illnesses, heart failure, and the like. When they passed, they tested positive for COVID. So, what happens? The hospital reports that they had a COVID death . . . even though the real cause wasn't actually from the disease. This was money-driven, plain and simple: more COVID care meant more federal funding for the hospital.

Numbers were skewed much higher than reality.

In other countries, however, the numbers were vastly skewed the other way. Many African countries had very little access to resources. A doctor in the country of Burundi even admitted that "There are zero cases in Burundi because there have been zero tests." There certainly were cases, and there certainly were deaths, but without the resources to test, there is no information to report.

All the numbers being reported were skewed one way or another. It will likely be years before anyone can truly analyze just how many lives were affected by the virus.

Throughout the fall, countries were taking even more measures to protect their citizens. Many of the Schengen countries were tightening up their borders—perhaps not locking them down completely but limiting access and doing health checks of those coming in.

The CDC announced that cruise ships once again must dock. Italy had mandatory testing of travelers. The country of Nepal reported a hundred thousand cases in one day. Spain declared a state of emergency, Belgium required that all elective procedures be halted, and India saw their eight millionth case.

France was once again locked down. Denmark exterminated seventeen million minks when it was discovered that a mutation of the virus could transmit from humans to animals.

By the beginning of November, fifty million cases had been announced worldwide.

A new "more transmissible" variant was discovered in the UK and in South Africa. Personal protective equipment was scarce, causing doctors in Kenya to strike. Nowhere was safe, and even Antarctica documented a case.

The virus was mutating, people were concerned, millions upon millions of people were infected, and nobody knew what was going on.

2020 came to a close, and things were looking worse than they did back in March when it all started.

CHAPTER 68

UPSIDE DOWN

In the tax planning world, just about everything was upside down as 2020 drew to a close.

Typically, most people's incomes follow a pattern. Their incomes will vary, usually slightly, but they do follow patterns, making their tax planning a little bit easier. However, 2020 was such an odd year that those patterns were vastly upset.

Many of our clients were past retirement age and relying on investments and Social Security for their income. This (simplified) example wasn't out of the ordinary when we looked at 2019 and 2020 side by side.

Jane is seventy-five years old. She has a sizable IRA, other investments, and Social Security income that provides a decent retirement for her. In 2019, a year when the stock market did very well, her income looked like this:

Social Security: $25,000

Investment Income: $5,000

Capital Gains: $40,000

IRA Required Minimum Distribution: $70,000

> Federal Taxable Income: $136,250 (85 percent Social
> Security taxable)

However, come 2020, her income looked like this:
  Social Security: $25,000
  Investment Income: $5,000
  Capital Gains: ($3,000) that is, a loss due to a bad year in
    the market
  IRA RMD: $0
  Federal Taxable Income: $2,000 (Social Security not
    taxable at this level)

Not many issues could come about from this, but there was one valuable—albeit time-consuming—opportunity.

Because her estimated taxes were based on previous years when her income was largely the same, she way overpaid taxes in 2020. In fact, if she had taken her RMD and then repaid it in full, she would have paid even more than necessary. Remember, IRA distributions generally come out with taxes withheld, but the IRS won't send those taxes back—instead, they're applied to the tax return filed after year-end.

So, here's a client who paid vastly more than what she owed because her current taxes were more-or-less nothing. Because she had little or no taxable income, she was in the perfect situation to convert her IRA into a ROTH IRA. That conversion would trigger taxes due on the converted amount, but since she was in such a low bracket, the taxes would be minimal.

To get that process started, however, we had to contact her financial advisors to determine the amount that could optimally be converted, and then to discover any gains that could be recognized in the no- or low-tax environment.

But we weren't done yet. Now that we had one oddball year for taxes, estimates for the next year were all screwed up. Very little tax was owed for 2020, and the 2021 taxes were based on the previous year's income. So when estimates were paid for a year that was (somewhat) back to normal, the estimates came in way too low. When it was time to file those 2021 returns, clients were upset that now they had to come up with cash to pay the remainder that was due.

And pretty much every client was calling in, asking questions. They all boiled down to, "Well, what do you think we should do?" They all had to be dealt with, they all needed answers, and they all took up just a little bit more time out of the completely filled-up day.

More drips into the already overflowing cup. There was no capacity, but all this had to be done before the end of the year to make sure conversions took place and stock market trades had settled before the year-end.

CHAPTER 69

ZOOM IN

At the end of December 2019, Zoom reported ten million daily users. Three months later, that number skyrocketed to two hundred million.

From the beginning of the pandemic, Zoom became a household name. Just about everyone knew what it was, as this software took off in popularity, leaving many of the other similar products, even those that had a much longer history, in the dust.

Now, just about every grandparent in America was figuring out Zoom or FaceTime in an effort to see their grandkids. And it wasn't just those intent on catching up with one another. Even my dad, in his nineties at the time, learned how to use FaceTime on his iPhone so we could see each other when we chatted.

Office meetings were being moved online, usually via Zoom. Client meetings were done on the phone or through Zoom instead of in person. Even office parties were held . . . through a screen. Companies were even doing virtual wine tastings—everyone would order the same bottle of wine, then log into the Zoom meeting and compare notes.

Throughout 2020, more and more people hopped online for their meetings. Those fortunate enough to hold stock in Zoom saw their portfolios increase dramatically. Shares of the stock went from the mid $60s per share in December 2019 up to over $550 per share in October 2020—nearly a 900 percent increase in a matter of months.

Despite the financial boom for the company, there was a serious side effect that came from all these online meetings. It turns out that Zoom burnout was negatively affecting people's mental health—the stress levels of sitting in a Zoom meeting were much higher than in face-to-face meetings.

As researchers dug into this issue, they discovered several reasons. These meetings, held from the comfort of our own homes (and often while wearing athletic shorts instead of suit pants), weren't designed like face-to-face meetings.

First, your camera is pointed at you. And your face shows up on the screen along with everyone else's face. But how many times have you gone into a meeting and set up a mirror in front of you? How often do you look at yourself while you're in a meeting? Constantly checking our appearance means our brains are working overtime, trying to focus on the meeting but also making sure we don't have a rogue hair, a booger hanging out, or that we're making a strange face.

Second, you're looking directly at everyone else's face. If you sit around a conference table with ten or twelve other people, half of them will be on the same side of the table as you. You don't look at all the faces at once. In addition, you're often looking down at notes, or watching the presentation, or looking at memes on your phone. Gazing into the eyes of a bunch of other people all at once is disconcerting—something our brains aren't wired for—and it puts us on edge.

Finally, when you are looking at a screen, paying attention to the speaker, and monitoring every other face (including your own), you tend to forget to blink. The brain is pulled in so many directions that the basics are essentially forgotten.

Somewhere along the way, "training" was established for how to use Zoom. Turn off the display for your own camera, use the presenter view so you only see one person at a time, and don't forget to blink. Much of that came far too late and was largely ignored by the masses, who were already inundated with information on a new way of living.

A growing number of people claimed that when COVID was over, they would never do another Zoom call as long as they lived.

CHAPTER 70

WARP 7

Back in the 1970s and '80s, I was quite the Trekkie. The license plate on my Fiat proudly declared "WARP 7." Project Warp Speed, which President Trump announced in 2020, however, did not have to do with deep space, Star Trek, or anything else science fiction related.

When Warp Speed was announced, roughly half the country thought it was actually just fiction. There was skepticism and concern—many flat-out believed it was not possible to safely make a vaccine in such a short amount of time. Hopefuls were on one side, skeptics on the other, and a lot of polarization in between.

On January 1, 2021, the US had over a hundred thousand COVID hospitalizations. It was the same day that the WHO granted emergency approval for Pfizer's vaccine in developing markets.

Around the world were many different brands of vaccines. All sought to do the same thing: slow and stop the spread of the disease. When vaccines were launched, some countries jumped on board right away, while others were slower to adapt.

By January 3, Israel had vaccinated 10 percent of its population. A few days later, the US saw four thousand deaths in a single day.

By January 14, Israel had vaccinated 20 percent of its population. A day later, the world surpassed two million COVID deaths.

Later that week, Turkey used China's Sinovac vaccine and gave over six hundred thousand shots. Germany saw one million people vaccinated.

By early February, UNICEF announced they would work with India's Serum Institute to produce 1.1 billion doses of the vaccine for use in low-income countries.

It appeared to be working, too. By the end of February, the WHO announced six consecutive weeks of declining cases around the globe . . . despite the fact that, at the same time, 2.5 million people had now died from the virus.

In the US, vaccines were rolled out in waves. First to those at the greatest risk, including healthcare workers, the elderly, and the otherwise compromised. As more and more vaccines were available, they opened up to the rest of the population. And then, the conspiracy theories started pouring in.

While Pfizer was developing one of the vaccines, Moderna was developing another. Rumors started to spread that Bill Gates developed COVID-19 and the Moderna vaccine as a means of controlling people and increasing his wealth. Many went as far as to say that the shot contained a microchip that would track and manipulate behavior.

Others firmly believed that the vaccine was racially motivated. Because it was developed to affect mRNA, the misinformation spread that it attacked those with specific racial DNA.

Along those lines, because this science was so misunderstood, many latched onto the false idea that the vaccine would alter your DNA.

The vaccine was claimed to cause infertility, make a person magnetic, or cause autism. Some of those claims have been around for any vaccine for years and years.

Claims that the vaccine would cause health problems and long-term complications abounded, and many people falsely believed that the variants of COVID we saw later in the year were a direct result of the virus mutating to avoid being "taken out" by the vaccine.

The truth was that the vaccines came to the public with far less testing than any other vaccination in history. They were also developed independently by many different companies, had a lot of funding to pay scientists for their hard work, and worked differently than the vast majority of vaccines out there.

In the end, there were people who had reactions to the vaccines. But there were billions of people around the world who were successfully vaccinated with no side effects.

CHAPTER 71

TROJAN HORSE

I remember when I was in eighth grade and student body elections were coming up. A handful of girls went around to some of the more popular boys and convinced them to run for class president. These guys were already popular, and I thought, "This is great. Certainly one of the best candidates will win!"

Little did we know that the girls had an ulterior motive. One of their friends had slipped onto the ballot, largely unnoticed—she was the only female candidate.

While the boys had split votes, the girls joined forces and voted for their friend. She easily won the election.

This is how I view California's Proposition 19, which passed on November 3, 2020. It quietly slipped onto the ballot at a time when the population was exhausted—accountants, especially—and it could get voted in without people raising a lot of noise.

Because those of us who work in the tax industry were tired, we had finished the regular tax season and the extended tax season, and we were still struggling to stay up-to-date with all the new laws and what they meant. We barely noticed this poorly drafted proposition. The holidays were coming, and we longed for a bit of respite.

So, what was the big deal? Under the old rules, California's Proposition 13, children could inherit property without a step-up in assessed value. For instance, if your parents bought an apartment complex decades ago for $800,000—the assessed value would still be based on $800,000 for tax purposes. This meant it cost roughly $10,000 per year in property taxes. Then, when they died or it was otherwise transferred to you, it would still be assessed at $800,000, even if the new value was $5,000,000.

The new Prop 19 got rid of that lower assessment transfer. Starting on February 15, 2021, property would be reassessed and taxed based on the value at the time of transfer. So, that $10,000 in property taxes jumped to $60,000 upon transfer—that $50,000 increase was forever.

Some of the bigger issues, however, were that the proposition was poorly worded, ambiguous, and altogether a huge burden for many of our clients. The Santa Clara County Assessor's website even talked about how terrible it was:

Proposition 19 was hastily passed by the legislature in less than a week and put on the November 2020 ballot. While it changed the state constitution it did not provide implementing statutes. Moreover, portions of the approved language changes are ambiguous, unclear and/or conflicting.[1]

There were only two fixes, two choices, that clients with property could do. They could either die before February 15 or they could transfer the property to their kids before that date. Not a

---

1. https://www.sccassessor.org/tax-savings/transferring-your-assessed-value/parent-to-child-2

great situation, no matter how you look at it, but it was complicated by even more COVID-related situations.

To do a property transfer, you needed two things: an attorney
to draw up the transfer documents, and an appointment at the
county clerk's office to submit the paperwork.

Attorneys who were available to handle this type of work were
few and far between—if you didn't already "have a guy," you probably weren't going to find one willing to draft up the paperwork
on such short notice. Not to mention that county offices were
all closed and only accepting people by appointment. So, good
luck getting in there to submit the paperwork, even if you had
an attorney who was able to put together the paperwork for you.

We also had just a few weeks to have the conversation with all
our clients who owned property like this, determine if they were
in the position to transfer it, and then make it all happen.

In our offices, we had a few clients who were able to follow
through on it. One was already in his eighties and was in the early
planning stages of transferring his property anyway. He had an
attorney he could use, his kids were older and responsible, and
we managed to get everything done in time. Conservative estimates put his (his kids') tax savings at well over a million dollars
over the course of their lifetime.

Our cups were already overflowing. Now, it was like we were
being waterboarded by that overflowing cup.

. . . Oh, is it tax season again?

CHAPTER 72

GRANDMA IS FACETIMING ME TO ASK WHY GRADUATION IS CAN-CELED

By the spring of 2021, vaccines had been rolled out across the US. As those who were at the most risk received their first doses, the opportunity for others to be vaccinated opened up. An issue now, however, was whether there were enough doses or you would stand in line and then never actually get your shot.

To solve that problem, the heavily populated areas of California came up with a system where you received a date to receive your first shot.

Ordinarily, I would never go in for non-emergency medical care in the middle of tax season. There was simply too much going on as an accountant, and I didn't have the time to take off. During this particular tax season, however, I did it twice.

In March 2021, I signed up online for an appointment to receive my first COVID vaccination shot. On that date, I stood in a line that seemed to be over a half-mile long. For the next few hours, we slowly inched our way forward. Upon reaching the front of the line, I received the first dose and my vaccine card. I scheduled a time and date four weeks out to get my second dose. In April of 2021, I stood in line yet again to receive the second dose of the COVID-19 vaccine.

Around the country, people were lining up to get these vaccines as millions were still anxious for life to get back to normal—it was now a year from the start of the pandemic.

Senior homes around the country were still locked down. Grandparents were becoming proficient with using FaceTime, and they were calling, wondering what was happening "on the outside."

Because they lived in a community residence, one positive case of COVID meant that the entire community would be locked down. Finally, when there were no more positive tests, it was another two weeks of quarantine before things could open up again. Then, another positive test would come along, and it would all get locked down once again.

Nobody really knew what was going on or if they needed to completely lock down like that. So they erred on the conservative side and kept the doors shut to protect the elderly.

I believe that years from now, study upon study will have been done about COVID, the social implications, the economic effects, and what really happened. Analysis will be done, and the number of people who never got to say goodbye to their aging parents and grandparents will be staggering.

In 2023, as this book is being written, we are only a couple of years out from the big lockdowns. And these memories of the nightmare that COVID put us through have already started to fade.

For many accountants, however, we were still in the thick of it, and only recently have we been able to let our guard down a bit and relax.

CHAPTER 73

HOLD YOUR HORSES

By the spring of 2021, COVID was a hot mess. It had been starting to look like everything was clearing up, as though the virus was about to be vanquished. Suddenly, it turned 180 degrees and cases spiked again. Panic ensued, lockdowns were re-established, and just as suddenly, it turned around again. It was like watching a tennis match and the emotional roller coaster to go along with it.

India, one of the most vaccinated countries in the world (and the country with the largest population), was down to fewer than ten thousand cases per day. As the newest variant of the virus spread, however, those cases did an about-face and rose quickly. On April 5, the country reported a hundred thousand new cases in a day. Less than a month later, they were reporting four hundred thousand cases in a single day.

Slovakia, having received the Sputnik V vaccine from Russia, announced they had concerns about the quality of the vaccine.

The Chinese CDC said their own vaccines weren't effective enough.

Over three million people had died from COVID by the middle of April 2021. Meanwhile, Sudan was planning to destroy sixty thousand doses of the vaccine because they had expired . . . the WHO said, "Woah, wait, don't do that!"

Many countries were kicking around the idea of vaccine passports—cards that showed you had been vaccinated and meant that you could travel freely without quarantining extensively upon entering another country. There was talk of it happening in the US, but the Biden administration denied any veracity to those claims.

And now, there were arguments over the vaccine patents. Companies that spent a lot of money developing the vaccines believed that they should be able to keep the patents and profit from the drug. Other people touted that it was for the good of humanity and nobody should hold a patent on something so necessary.

By the middle of May, the Delta variant (B.1.617) that had plagued India (causing infection rates of greater than 20 percent of the population) was spreading around the world. It wasn't as deadly as the original but was just as contagious. The EU announced a travel ban to India to help limit exposure.

Then, tourist season began.

After missing out on the tourist season of 2020, dozens of countries around the world were hurting economically. They relied on that money to be flowing throughout the spring, summer, and into the fall—another year without tourists spending money in their countries could have incredibly long-lasting effects. So, despite the Delta variant and infection rates spiking, they were opening their borders and asking people to come.

Greece reopened its borders, and Italy lifted its mandatory quarantine requirements.

The EU agreed that US citizens who showed proof of vaccination were once again welcome to come visit. By the time May ended and the summer began, over one billion vaccines had been given worldwide, and the daily new cases were on a sharp decline. People around the world believed that this was the end and we were finally wiping out the virus.

But while travel bans were being lifted, some countries were tightening up. On June 19, Uganda reimposed their forty-two-day lockdown, as their new daily cases had surged to an all-time high.

By the end of the month, Turkey had lifted all COVID curfews, the Philippine president threatened to arrest Filipinos who refused the vaccine, and quarantine-free travel between Australia and New Zealand was suspended after a surge in new cases in Sydney.

Some countries were seeing a decline in cases, and they were anxious and ready to open up. Others were seeing a surge in cases, so they tightened restrictions and locked down again. Back and forth, like a tennis ball, as one opened and another closed.

Slowly, we were coming out of it, but just as it looked like things were getting better, a surge in new cases hit.

CHAPTER 74

WAKE ME WHEN IT'S OVER

Congress was still moving full steam ahead. They were still passing laws much faster than in the past, and those laws were being implemented with very little—or sometimes no—guidelines on how they were supposed to be interpreted or put into action.

Every time one of those acts was implemented, or even just a portion of an act, it created a ton of work for accountants and tax preparers. As you have seen with all the laws that had been passed to this point, they seemed straightforward, but dozens of situations made them messy.

In 2021, the American Rescue Plan Act was passed. Part of this plan included advanced payments for the child tax credit, and a third round of stimulus money that went out to all tax-payers. Of course, whenever people see something from the IRS, they get a little worried, a little nervous.

Sometimes, that money hit their bank account and they just said, "Cool!" and then moved on. But more often, money came into their bank account and immediately, they picked up the phone to ask their accountant what was going on.

That third round of stimulus money came with stipulations and guidelines, just like the other two did. This one, however, gave each taxpayer $1,400 and each dependent $1,400. But because of the income limitations, some individuals weren't eligible for this round of money—even if they received both of the stimulus payments in 2020.

If filing a joint tax return and the couple was making over $150,000, they would see their stimulus reduced; if they were making over $160,000, no 2021 stimulus was available.

The big difference in this round, however, was regarding the payment that went to dependents. It included college students and other adult dependents, not just children under the age of seventeen.

Determining eligibility was again based on the last tax return filed.

Every client had a different scenario. Every client had questions. Every client wondered, "What if we set it up this way . . ." and every call just kept dripping into the overflowing cup.

CHAPTER 75

TWO-WEEK RULE

Many years ago, my wife and I decided we would have a two-week rule. With six kids between the two of us, the rule was designed so that anyone could come to visit, but they could stay a maximum of two weeks.

Naturally, we weren't always hard and fast with this rule. When our daughter Amy and her husband came back from Thailand, where they worked as missionaries, we allowed them to stay a bit longer. There were a number of circumstances that led to that decision.

Amy was pregnant with their second baby. The first was born in Thailand, and there were no issues. Of course, we weren't in a pandemic at the time. The second baby was due in the summer of 2020, and they decided to come home to have the baby so they didn't have to worry about shutdowns or hospitals being maxed out with COVID patients.

Since they didn't want to travel later in the pregnancy, they decided to come in advance to provide enough leeway that no complications would arise while traveling. We weren't about to make them go find a short-term rental, so naturally, we waived the two-week rule for this particular trip.

Shortly after they arrived, COVID swept across the country and across the world. The Thai government banned all travel into the country by those who were not Thai citizens—even if they had lived in the country for many years prior.

So now, Amy, her husband, their firstborn, and soon the second-born were guests at our house indefinitely.

They wanted to get back to Thailand, but it was incredibly difficult to navigate any websites and get solid information on the procedures. The couple would spend hours every day, searching online and trying to figure out the rules, trying to determine which rules were the latest ones, and make their best "guess" as to when they would head back home.

That two-week rule was blown out of the water when their visit lasted for over six months.

Finally, Thailand made Phuket a COVID-free zone. They were allowing tourists to come in (and spend tourism money). Everyone was tested before entering and before leaving. Any Thai citizen who worked in the COVID-free zone had to quarantine for two weeks before they could enter.

The young family took a chance and headed back to Thailand. They were able to get into the country but then had to sit in a hotel room for ten days. Husband, wife, and two babies in a hotel room—no ability to leave or see anything for nearly two weeks.

CHAPTER 76

MY BODY MY CHOICE

The US is supposed to be a country with freedom of choice. We can choose what we feel is best for our own health and prosperity. However, as the vaccinations rolled out, many mandates were borderline infringing on the constitution. Many people had concerns about the vaccine, they weren't sure how safe it was or if there were long-term side effects, and they wanted to wait to be vaccinated or never be vaccinated at all.

Coming down the line, however, were many legal mandates that said you had to be vaccinated or sanctions could be imposed. Combine that with the polarity that was already rampant in the US, and we split into two castes. There are the unvaxxed on one side and the vaxxed on the other side. It appeared as though businesses might follow suit: vaxxed-only restaurants, unvaxxed-only grocery stores, vaxxed and unvaxxed shopping hours . . . Around the world, it wasn't much better.

In July, the EU issued travel passes. You had to prove you were vaccinated in order to receive your travel pass. Soon,

Greece, France, and Italy mandated vaccines for all essential workers—some states and departments in the US wanted to deploy a similar rule. Any government worker would need to be vaccinated or would be forced to undergo weekly testing.

France had health passes—a clean bill of health would get you a bit more freedom to move about. This was despite the CDC warnings that said you could still catch and spread COVID; were health passes really doing much?

When summer was ending, the Biden administration issued an executive order that mandated vaccinations for all federal employees and put forth a plan to require all employers with one hundred employees or more to ensure their workforce was vaccinated.

People were looking for booster shots. It had been more than six months since the initial group was vaccinated, and boosters were now available. However, the FDA insisted that people should hold off while the unvaccinated had a chance to receive their first shots.

The government continued to push for more vaccines, especially by those they employed. As we entered into the winter and then the spring of 2022, the military started to follow through on their commitment to discharge enrolled personnel who were unwilling to be vaccinated. By the time all was said and done, 3,400 troops would be involuntarily separated from service.

Our country was being pulled apart based on whether a person had chosen to receive the vaccination. And the government was trying to push everyone back together by requiring them to become vaccinated—many people, both vaccinated and unvaccinated, declared this to be in bad form and possibly unconstitutional.

CHAPTER 77

WHERE ARE ALL THE PEOPLE?

Going into COVID, our accounting firm had twenty-four people on staff. By the end of 2021, half of them had left to pursue other opportunities—all but three of them leaving public accounting for good.

Because, at the end of 2021, we were still working on 2020 taxes. Things were taking that long to make sure we had everything situated in what we believed was the true intention of all the new laws. Over the last few months, however, CARES Act money had been trickling into accounts. Some of it, such as the $300 advanced payment for child tax credits, was hitting bank accounts, and clients didn't say anything—they just spent the money.

This money, however, wasn't a gift. It wasn't a stimulus like the others. This money was an advanced payment for a credit they would have otherwise received the following tax season. What many didn't realize was that because they received it early, that meant they wouldn't receive it later . . . and then they would be on the phone with their accountant, trying to figure out why their tax refund was so small.

Early on in my career, I realized that when people receive more money than expected, they often don't question it. However, if they receive less than expected, they demand answers. For example, if an employee gets their paycheck on a Friday afternoon and it's $5 or $10 less than what they thought it would be, they're mad. They don't go home until they have figured out what was going on. But the other end of the spectrum changes their reaction considerably.

I had a client who, year after year, would receive the same paycheck with the same pay, and everything was more-or-less equal. Consistently, every year, she would receive a $10,000 tax return after her taxes were filed.

One year, she received her returns that showed she *owed* $10,000.

Naturally, she had questions and brought them to my attention. I scrutinized her returns, and we talked for a long time—were there unexpected earnings, inheritance money, something? Finally, I noticed that her W2 showed that her federal withholding had changed—it was set up to withhold $20,000 less than the year before. The only way that would happen is if she had filled out a new W4 and told her employer to change withholdings.

This client said nothing had changed and there was no big bonus or anything like that. The best we could figure out was that halfway through the year, she had an annual cost-of-living pay increase. And someone had accidentally changed the withholding going forward. In a biweekly pay period, that would mean hundreds of extra dollars per paycheck . . . but she never questioned it. She never asked why she suddenly had this extra money that eventually added up to $20,000 extra coming to her.

The same thing happened with that advanced payment of the child tax credits. People saw that the IRS was sending them $300 per month, and they didn't care. They just spent the money.

Now, as the year wrapped up and we progressed into early 2022, we started getting calls. And with each one, we had to explain the law. We had to explain why they received this money early and why they wouldn't get it later. Every client got a crash course on credits (which are different from deductions) and how their tax return would be smaller because they received thousands of dollars in advance.

Many would then ask, "Well, what if I didn't want this?" And we would ask, "Well, did you get the letter? Did you open the letter? Did you go online and opt out?" The system was set up so that you could opt out . . . but if you didn't, you just kept receiving those payments.

Most of the people calling didn't understand what was going on, and even after we thoroughly explained it, they still didn't understand a fairly complicated tax matter.

Of course, this ended up with another mess on their returns. At the beginning of each tax season, we send a questionnaire that asks about their situation. For 2022, we updated the form to ask about those advanced child tax credits because we needed the number for planning—if it wasn't reported correctly, the tax return would be flagged and not accepted by the IRS. Most people had already lost the 1099 that came, and as their accountants, we had the joy of spending extra hours trying to track down those amounts.

FUN IN THE SUN ...
WHERE ARE ALL THE PEOPLE?

Island life was vastly different from life on the mainland. If Hawaii, or another island state or nation, were to suffer from a COVID outbreak, it could quickly zap all resources and devastate the population.

To help protect the islands, Hawaii implemented stringent travel measures to visit. Starting in March 2020, visitors who could actually get to Hawaii had to self-quarantine for fourteen days. Those measures were lessened over time as vaccines became available, but even in March 2022, self-quarantining measures were still in place.

When Mark passed away in the spring of 2020, I was tasked with selling his timeshares. Even in the best of times, selling a timeshare is not easy to do—during COVID, those sales were next to impossible.

As of this writing, more than three years later, there is still a final Hawaiian timeshare that I basically can't give away. Mark purchased it for between $30,000 and $40,000—now it was on the market for $3,000, and there was no interest. It was like selling ice cubes in a snowstorm; when there was no demand, there was no sale.

Accountants, in general, hate timeshares anyway. They work great for people who want to go to the same place at the same time of year, every year. They serve a purpose, but the finances around them tend to be a nightmare. Then, if you want to sell one during a pandemic, forget about it!

Most of the time, you buy into them through a ritzy sales process. The owner will fly you out to the spot, you spend a week or two at the timeshare, and then you're sold on the idea that you can come and use your timeshare every single year.

During a pandemic, when people own timeshares they can't use, they want to get rid of them. They want to get their money out of them and use it for something they love or, at the very least, spend the money on something they can actually use. Quickly, the market was flooded with timeshares—and it remains flooded even now that quarantine and travel restrictions to Hawaii have been lifted.

THE HAVES AND THE HAVE NOTS

Around the world, countries that have access to vaccines are the Haves. But plenty of poorer countries do not have access to the vaccines, and they are the Have Nots. The long-term effects of these countries not being able to vaccinate their citizens will have a ripple effect for years. I believe that when the dust settles and we are finally able to go back and analyze what happened on a global economic scale, the wealth gap between countries and classes of people will have widened dramatically.

The end of 2021 was coming. And a number of countries were realizing the idea of "Zero-COVID," that is, the idea that they could achieve days and weeks with absolutely no cases, was a pipe dream. Now, it was minimized and expected that there would always be some cases at any given time.

Meanwhile, Western countries (Haves) were opening up as significant portions of the population were vaccinated and had received boosters. Now, many of the other countries (Have Nots) were getting vaccines for the first time. In the middle of October

2021, the US sent seventeen million doses of the J&J vaccine to the Africa Union. Later that month, BioNTech announced plans to build an mRNA COVID-19 vaccine manufacturing facility in Rwanda and Senegal.

This came after reports from the WHO that said six of seven cases in Africa went undetected. Meaning that all the numbers were dramatically skewed—true cases could be well over fifty million.

The UK caught on and said they would send twenty million vaccines before 2021 came to a close, and Taiwan donated 150,000 doses to Somaliland.

Through the first months of 2022, the Pan-American Health Organization delivered a hundred million vaccines to Latin America and throughout the Caribbean. The US announced that vaccine assistance would increase to eleven African countries.

Meanwhile, the US was largely opened back up (outside of a handful of areas, including California). The problem employers were facing then, however, was that despite the number of people who were laid off while in the throes of the pandemic, very few were returning to work. Claims of "Nobody wants to work anymore!" abounded, and few people knew why.

Again, when the dust settles, we'll know what really happened. It is, however, agreed upon that two economic factors played a big role.

Wages remained low. Despite the job openings, many businesses hadn't increased their wages by much. Since the beginning of 2022, that has changed considerably. But coming out of the pandemic, "nobody wanted to work anymore" because wages weren't satisfactory.

But really, the fact that they had money already played a factor in whether they could even hold off for those better-paying jobs. Boosted unemployment benefits and several rounds of stimulus (as well as diminished entertainment opportunities) meant that households across the country were flush with cash. In the middle of 2021, the typical US household had 50 percent more cash than two years prior.

Lower-income families were making out even better than higher-income families—when you look at their cash as a percentage of what they had before. Those considered to be lower income were up 70 percent higher than two years prior.

So, with all this cash and the desire to not work for what they considered to be too low of wages, they were able to live better than they had before without working.

Why return to work when your net worth and lifestyle are significantly better than they were pre-COVID?

CHAPTER 80

BUT, BUT, BUT

A law, changed in 2021, slipped by largely unnoticed. This law stated that if you received $600 or more through a third-party settlement organization (like eBay or Amazon) in a single transaction, you would receive a 1099-K. In other words, you would have to report that income to the IRS. We were all told about it, we all knew it was coming, but the implementation was still a couple of years away, so who cares?

A law was already in place that required receipts and a 1099-K for taxpayers who received $20,000 in aggregate payments and two hundred transactions—in other words, most real businesses out there were doing this. They already received a 1099-K every January. But this new law dropped that threshold from $20,000 to $600 with no minimum number of transactions.

Now, as 2022 was getting underway, accountants and the IRS were gearing up to implement this new law. Suddenly, it was in every media outlet across the country. People were sharing their concerns on social media and creating petitions to keep the government out of their bank accounts.

After reading the articles online or hearing the news reports, people started calling our office. Questions abounded. Clients were asking, "So, if I sell my kid's bicycle for $600, I'll have to receive a 1099 for it and then report it on my taxes?"

The answer: "Yep, perhaps. At this point in time, that's how it's being interpreted."

The biggest issue, for the accountants, anyway, wasn't that the government was trying to monitor how much cash was coming into accounts. It was that hardly anyone had the information necessary to properly report this stuff. People who sold personal items almost always did so at a loss. They didn't track their costs, marketing efforts, etc. In the long run, it would be a lot of purchases at a higher price, sold at a lower price, so no income. All reported on a Schedule C—more work for accountants and more hassle for the clients.

You may remember the uproar about this new law. And ultimately, Congress quietly pushed the implementation date out by a year. If they hadn't, it would have required many new forms, complicated updates to already-complicated software, and many more hours of work.

Before the end of 2022, the law had been pushed back. But we had all already prepped for it and we had put in the time required to make sure we wouldn't be caught off-guard (or were at least *less* off-guard). Those were hours of prep time that we didn't have, we didn't get paid for, and only added to that overflowing cup that was drowning out a large part of the tax preparer industry.

CHAPTER 81

CABIN FEVER

Like so many other people, my wife and I wanted to get out and travel. We longed for someplace other than our house and our immediate neighborhood.

Travel for many, however, was still pretty dangerous at the beginning of 2022. For those who were vaccinated, there was a bit less risk. However, there were plenty who couldn't be vaccinated. They may have had underlying health issues or autoimmune diseases. This made travel not only difficult but also dangerous. The last thing you wanted to do was put yourself at risk by merely using the bathroom at a gas station.

Not that you really could—around California, many of the public restrooms were still closed.

We decided that instead of bemoaning the fact that we couldn't travel as much as we wanted to, we instead purchased an RV. Then, we knew exactly who had been in the bathroom (only us), exactly when it had been sanitized, and we didn't even have to eat dinner at a crowded restaurant.

We weren't, however, the first to think of this idea. There was a big demand for RVs by people who wanted to travel but with minimized concerns and worries about getting out. So, we got on a waitlist.

We were fortunate enough to get on that waitlist before the supply chain issues really started coming down the line. When those hit, the waitlist got even longer as fewer and fewer RVs became available, but the demand for them only increased.

Driving without worrying about the location of the next open and clean bathroom was amazing. We had the opportunity to head north into rural Oregon and see our kids and grandkids whom we hadn't seen in over a year. We didn't have any worries about a potentially germ-infested hotel, and even while visiting, we had the opportunity, should it arise, to isolate from anyone else who appeared to be getting sick.

This really was quite the boon.

Even outside of COVID scares, if you want to minimize worry when you travel, a small RV is a spectacular way to see the country from the comfort of your own "home."

CHAPTER 82

WEARY — COULD IT REALLY GET ANY WORSE?

The Winter Olympics came to Beijing in early February 2022. The only way to describe those games was that the whole situation was just weird.

A number of events were significantly changed. And the athletes were different than what you might have been expecting. Some of the top-tier athletes tested positive shortly before the games began, so countries had to send the next-best athletes. The result wasn't a bad Olympics but one that was just different than what we expected.

The National Hockey League decided that it was too dangerous to send all their top athletes overseas at that time. Instead, the NHL bowed out, and college athletes and minor league players represented the US on the ice.

Besides a difference in talent, the athletes who did attend were required to live in a "closed-loop management system." A what? Yeah, it was a bubble. The entire set of residents of Olympic

Village were required to live in strange housing—if someone did test positive for COVID, they were moved to a quarantined hotel that many described as a living hell.

Before the games were even over, global deaths from COVID soared past the six-million-lives mark. Talks resumed about how authoritarian countries should be banned from participating, with thirty-five countries calling for Russian athletes to be unable to compete. In the winter of 2022, in what was called a "state-sponsored doping scheme," Russian athletes were "banned." This only had them compete under the Russian Olympic Committee instead of the Russian flag, and it wasn't a complete ban on the authoritarian nation.

Here in North America, a Freedom Convoy was moving through Canada. Ontario announced that truck drivers would get quarantined for fourteen days upon entering the province. To avoid this, you had to prove that you had received both the first round of the vaccine and the second follow-up dose. Naturally, truckers in the US and Canada saw this as an infringement on their freedom of choice, and there was a huge movement to protest. Miles upon miles of freeways were blocked as truckers did a "sit-in" and refused to move.

Some of the biggest news events were taking our focus away from COVID at that time.

Before February 2022 had even wrapped up, Russia invaded Ukraine. Media outlets around the world all but dropped the "old news" of COVID, and now the focus was on why Russia was invading, why Ukraine was fighting back, and speculation on what the outcome of this war would be. Hint: a year and a half later, that war was still going on.

Even with the war commanding the world's attention, COVID was silently raging on.

Hong Kong's unvaccinated elderly residents were hit hard, and they surged to the top of the "daily deaths" list. China placed a number of cities under lockdown due to the Omicron variant making its rounds throughout the cities. It was so bad that Disneyland closed the doors to its Shanghai resort.

Shanghai, in an effort to curb the spread of this new variant, administered tests to all twenty-five million residents.

The first quarter of 2022 wrapped up, and COVID was still very much defining the world.

CHAPTER 83

COURT TV

Most people's accountants know more about their financial lives than just about anyone else. For some people, their accountant knows more about their finances than they even do.

That means if a couple goes through a divorce, they tap into the financial expert in their lives to help get everything sorted out. The accountant has a detailed history of everything financial that has happened in the couple's lives going back for years and years—oftentimes before they were even married.

I was helping a client go through a divorce (as their accountant). But early in 2022, all the courts were still closed. You could hardly even get into the building to collect the right documents, let alone visit with a judge. It was all still happening through Zoom. Truly a bizarre experience trying to navigate the difficult legal court proceedings but not actually being there in person.

Eventually, things opened back up and you could enter the courts again. Of course, this was the government, and they had bureaucracy to follow. There were rules on masks, distancing, protocols, and more. Depending on whether you were dealing with a local, state, or federal court, these protocols could vary considerably—there really was no way of knowing what to expect until you arrived at the courthouse.

California passed Proposition 47 back in 2014. This law made it far easier for people to get away with petty theft. If the value of the goods a person stole was less than $950, it would be counted as a misdemeanor instead of a felony. With jails and prisons overflowing, however, often no arrest was made—instead, the thief was given a notice to appear.

During COVID, things got even more messed up. For misdemeanors, those who actually were arrested, their bail went to $0. Evictions were put on hold for missing rent—all eviction hearings went away. For months upon months, a person could live in a home without paying rent, and the landlord couldn't do anything about it other than accept the financial loss. Even when evictions were reinstated, everything in the court system had changed and delays meant even more months of waiting until the proper eviction protocol could be followed.

It wasn't just in California, either. There were reports around the country about people brazenly walking off with goods from stores with no fear of consequences. Wearing a mask protected their identity, and nobody questioned someone wearing a mask now. So they could do as the criminals did recently in Tucson, Arizona. Criminals backed up their truck near the entrance to a sporting goods store, walked out with whatever they wanted, and drove off as calm as could be.

Crime, especially in many of the more liberal states, was already getting out of control. COVID, and post-COVID, it has gotten even worse.

CHAPTER 84

IS IT OVER YET?

Throughout 2022, we kept wondering, "Is this thing over yet?" The vast majority of the country had opened up—not California, though. That winter, California was hit with some of the worst flooding that we had seen in recent history.

Those floods affected a significant portion of the population. So much so that we were trying to deal with the aftermath as we approached tax season. Who would have thought that another major problem would affect our lives as we tried to prepare taxes!

The IRS stepped in to save the day once again. First, they moved Tax Day out one month until May. Then they moved it out again—the deadline to file 2022 taxes as a California citizen wasn't until October 2023. That sounded like great news, but it looked all too much like the confusing mess that happened when the tax deadline was changed in 2020. All those same questions came pouring in once again.

When were estimates due? What about foreign taxes? What about vacations for accountants—if we could actually take one this year?

If you lived in California, you likely received a notice (or at least read about it in the media) that you didn't have to file until October. There was no need to file an extension, there were no penalties for paying later, and you didn't owe anything; just move that deadline out six months later than usual. Our company has a "best practices" policy that says any time we need to file later than the normal Tax Day, we file that extension, whether it is required or not.

That simple act of covering our backsides spurred even more phone calls. Why did we do that?

Now, keep in mind that our firm isn't just a California firm. Many accountants have clients that come to them from all over the US. Our firm even has offices in Arizona, a state that wasn't hit by any major natural disasters and thus was not privy to the extended filing season.

Even those who did live in California but had income that came from another state were left wondering what to do. One of our clients received income from Connecticut. Connecticut wasn't shut down or delayed, so taxes for that state were still due in April . . . and the rest of their return wasn't due until October. So, do you file an extension for both states, file one in April and one in October, or just power through and get everything done in April?

Even then, you have the mess of going through every client's files to see who filed in another state in past years, then talking to them to see if they had income in another state in 2021. All for the sake of answering: When do you actually file?

To top it all off, major legislation was passed called IRC 174. It involved research or experimental (R&E) expenses that were to be amortized over a period of years. Every conference, every webinar, and every town hall brought it up—without any idea as to what would actually happen.

This law expired at the end of 2021. But everyone had expected it to be renewed for 2022. But there was no guidance on it, no word on the street, and nothing but radio silence from Congress. Instead of just not dealing with it, most accountants planned and acted as though it would be renewed.

The 2021 tax season came and went. Then the 2022 tax season came and went. We still didn't know if this thing would be retroactively renewed; nobody had heard anything yet.

The overflowing cup was drowning accountants . . . something had to change.

SUMMARY OF SECTION VI

We sped up for our final section of this book—things kept moving, kept changing, and kept us on our toes. Unless we wanted to extend into many hundreds of pages, it simply wasn't necessary to detail everything that happened "after" COVID.

COVID's effects, however, lingered on long after many states and countries opened back up. The WHO officially declared the pandemic to be "done" in May 2023—over three years after it was officially declared a pandemic.

Throughout 2021 and 2022, the lingering effects of the tax laws that were hastily (and necessarily) passed were still on our plates. We still had to deal with the fallout and go back and "fix" tax returns when the interpretation of the laws was discovered. Even to this day, some of those laws aren't fully defined. And we may not know the full effects for several more years.

It was 800 days of work for me. 800 days of trying to keep my head above water without taking a vacation day.

Let's hope we don't have to deal with that again. Despite all that has happened in the accounting world during COVID and beyond, I know it is still a wonderful and much-needed profession, and I hope to be part of the solution to ensure accountants are ready for the continued changes that are sure to come.

EPILOGUE

It is now fall 2023. Over three and a half years have passed since the beginning of the pandemic. The world is a different place today than it was in 2019. Some things seem similar. A presidential campaign is ramping up. Divisiveness prevails. Heatwaves and wildfires headline the news.

Other events are new. The war in Ukraine rages on. NATO is expanding. The economy seems uncertain.

COVID seems to be in the rear-view mirror. But the view out the front windshield feels cloudy.

The accounting profession lost over 20 percent of accountants in the pandemic. I suspect most just got tired. I'm tired too. In late 2022, I sold my remaining partnership interest to my partner. This was the plan all along, but I accelerated it by many years. Many factors brought me to this decision, but mostly I think I just felt tired. I continue to work for the firm and am fortunate to be able to focus on the parts of the profession that I love . . . working with clients in particular.

The demand for accountants continues to grow and I believe will increase significantly in the next few years. But change will be required to meet this demand for talented accounting professionals. The demands of the profession and the wants for work-life balance are on divergent paths.

I recently read that the shortage of accountants in industry (e.g., corporate accountants—not those who work with the public) was threatening the timeliness of SEC filings. The IRS is scheduled to receive $87 billion in additional funding (that means more hiring). The federal government is certain to start audits of all that free money they dispensed during the pandemic; those audits will require accountants to audit and represent the recipients.

Salary increases have already begun. But by itself, increased compensation will not fill the gap. I don't believe technology will, either. For the forty years I have worked in the accounting profession, there has been a constant "cloud" over the profession that technology would replace us. My experience has been that the technology has consistently resulted in a *greater need for more* accountants.

For the global economy to grow, we need more accounting professionals. But the pipeline (universities supplying graduates with accounting degrees) is not keeping up.

Just as the subtitle to this book (*Over 300,000 Accountants Quit During the Pandemic—Here's Our Story*) describes how the situation got so bad, I believe the solution will be by thousands of little things. A little more efficiency here, a new process there, a few more people, a few ideas to save time, and so on until it all adds up.

I stated in the Prologue that I hope to be a part of the solution. To offer some of those little solutions, I am launching a program to educate accountants, clients, and the public about how they can stay afloat. This program is designed to be a resource and information center for anyone who wants to be able to keep their head above water when tax changes come down the pipeline.

The town hall meetings that I talked about in this book were a good start, and they helped stave off a ton of anxiety and worry. To help revitalize the world of accounting, my program seeks to provide that much value on an ongoing basis.

It's called Rx4tax, and it will launch in late 2023.

P.S. Mark's last timeshare, in Maui, Hawaii, sold in October 2023. You may recall that Maui was the site of devastating wildfires in August 2023. Fingers crossed that the sale will be finalized by early spring 2024.

P.P.S. Tax Day in 2023 was supposed to be October 16. On the morning of the sixteenth, the IRS gave most California preparers and taxpayers another month. On the same day, after close of business (5 p.m.), the California Franchise Tax Board (FTB) made the same announcement . . . another month! The government did it to us again.

ACKNOWLEDGMENTS

Thank you to the wonderful tax team of seniors, managers, and partners at Deloitte during my tenure there (San Francisco) from 1982 to 1984. They instilled a love for the profession that I am forever thankful for.

The AICPA's creation of the Town Hall in 2020 was a real lifesaver for me. Their dedicated staff must have worked tirelessly to develop the content that kept us up-to-date weekly during the pandemic and saved us hours and hours of work. Eric's voice was a comfort to thousands of us struggling our way through the pandemic.

To the IRS employees who worked as hard as we did and who wrote laws and provided guidance under the most strenuous circumstances. I don't think anyone could have possibly imagined the quantity of legislation enacted during the pandemic . . . in fact, I still don't see how it happened.

To the many accountants I have worked with over the years. They are the most dedicated and loyal people I know—loyal to their clients, employers, and the profession.

To our many clients for their patience during the pandemic. I know it was frustrating at times. Thank you for being the most wonderful people to work with and to get to know.

To accountants everywhere who did their part to keep the economy functioning during the pandemic and for all their ideas, counsel, and friendship during these trying years.

ABOUT THE AUTHOR

Greg Hock began his accounting career in 1982 with one of the "big eight" firms in San Francisco. He has been self-employed in public practice since 1985. His firm grew to twenty-four staff members in 2020 when the pandemic hit. He sold his partnership interest in 2022 and is currently consulting with his prior firm. He resides in California with his wife, Cheryl, and their elderly dog and cat.

Greg launched Rx4tax in late 2023. These vodcasts will enable the public to use their accountants' time more effectively by understanding when to reach out, and when not to reach out, with questions. His hope is to start a process to decrease stress in the accounting profession and increase the attractiveness of the profession for younger potential accountants.